THE PSYCHOLOGY OF THE SAINTS

BY

HENRI JOLY

WITH PREFACE AND NOTES BY

G. TYRRELL, S.J.

AUTHOR'S PREFACE

HAVING treated successively of the psychology of the inferior animals,[1] of the psychology of great men,[2] and of the psychology of criminals,[3] I now come to the psychology of the saints.

We may ask: Are all these different psychologies utterly distinct one from the other? Is instinct an occult possession and crime a phenomenon standing quite by itself, a thing apart, the offspring of a deviation or spontaneous retrogression of the human race? Is the great man a mysterious gift of the Unconscious or the sudden incarnation of a spirit which sets at defiance all attempts at analysis? Is the saint a being in whom a miraculous agency has completely ousted and supplanted nature?—I have, in turn, endeavoured to combat every one of these notions.

There is one other theory, however, to which I am quite as unwilling to subscribe, and that is the theory that all manifestations of the human faculties, from the lowest even to the very highest, are produced by the blind and automatic action of our inferior powers. According to this idea, man is

---

[1] *L'instinct, ses rapports avec la vie et avec l'intelligence*, 2nd edition. Thorin, *L'homme et l'animal*, 3rd edition. Hachette.

[2] *Psychologie des grands hommes*, 2nd ed. Hachette.

[3] *Le crime*, 4th ed. *La France criminelle*, 3rd ed. *Le combat contre le crime.* 2nd ed. L. Cerf.

AUTHOR'S PREFACE

nothing better than an animal of a rather more complicated nature than the rest; crime is a disease; and genius and sanctity merely striking and, more often than not, fantastic exhibitions of the pride, ambition, self-deception and restlessness inherent in our nature.

No—great men and little, we are all of us formed out of the same clay and the same spirit is breathed into each one of us. We stand, as it were, on different steps of the same ladder, which springs from one and the same nature and reaches up to one and the same God.—We may aggravate the original weakness of our nature by yielding to it, or we may use the help offered to us and so develop all the potential strength and beauty it possesses, but whichever course we take, we can never completely destroy a single one of the features of our complex humanity. No matter how degenerate on the one hand, or perfect on the other, they may become, our fellow-men never fail to be objects of warning or encouragement to us. The resemblance we bear to one another affords us the means, while it teaches us the necessity, of applying the lesson to ourselves. It is under the influence of this conviction that the following essay has been written.[1]

[1] During the course of this work, I have often been obliged to treat of very difficult subjects. I wish to express my gratitude to M. Monier, Superior of the *École des Hautes Études ecclesiastiques*, who kindly revised my proof-sheets and placed his great theological learning, as well as his literary experience, at my disposal.

PREFACE

BESIDES the official dogmatic teaching of the Christian Church which can be reduced to a comparatively small compass there is a great mass of traditional beliefs, historical and religious, which she preserves with reverence and respect, not as in any sense setting her seal on every item of which it is composed, but because, as representing the "folk-lore," so to say, of the faithful at large, it has a critical value not final or decisive, but of an importance varying with the subject in hand. It is, we might say, a *nidus* from which matter is drawn from time to time to be subjected to the severer methods of criticism, and rejected or accepted according to the verdict. Taken as a whole, it contains a mingling of truth and error, as does every similar body of tradition; but for this reason to despise it or deny it all critical value would be to cast away the gold together with the ore. It can be trusted safely and usefully if its claims are rightly understood; for it does not pretend to be a mirror of facts, but only of subjective impressions and beliefs concerning facts. We cannot at once pass by inference from "It is said" to "It is"; yet "It is said" has an undoubted critical value under due conditions.

PREFACE

Hagiography is occupied with a large part of this body of Christian tradition; but until comparatively recent years, little had been done to sift the chaff from the grain in this department, beyond what was needed for the processes of canonisation. In the ages of faith—as they were called—there was a matter-of-course acceptance of much that we call marvellous; while in the succeeding age of unfaith there was an equally matter-of-course rejection of the same; but in neither case was there much discrimination attempted. But with the birth and growth of the historical and inductive methods, as well as with a more positive study of the rarer and abnormal phenomena of psychology, the "Acta Sanctorum" have acquired a new value and interest for the scientist and historian which must necessarily issue in results eventually advantageous to piety and religion.

One by one the strange facts recorded in saints' lives which were scouted by the hot-headed scepticism of a century ago and considered to discredit all hagiography, are now recognised as instances of well-known psychological manifestations. It is little to the purpose that they are explained as due to hypnosis, thought-transference, expectant attention, or other "word-causes"; the point is that, the philosophy which once denied these things as superstitions, is now convicted of superstition in that very denial.

The tendency of this reaction to explain all the phenomena in question by purely physiological or psychological laws needs to be counteracted by a

PREFACE

sounder criticism which shall fix the limits of what may be so explained, and shall assign to Nature the things that are Nature's and to God the things that are God's; and this is the task to which M. Joly addresses himself in the little volume which is here presented to the public in English dress.

It will, however, serve a no less important end if it enables educated Catholics to approach the lives of the saints with a more intelligent sympathy. The spiritual benefit derived from that study depends obviously on the applicability of their example to our own case; and this again, on the resemblance we see between their nature and circumstances and our own. It is this that spurs men to emulate their betters in the various walks of life,—a desire to equal or approach them, as well as a belief in the possibility of the enterprise. When the saints are set before us rather as wonderful than lovable; when we have no conception of the process of their spiritual evolution, how from rudiments of sanctity which are in us all, and by the aid of resources and faculties which we all possess, they obtained a result so different; until we have learnt to set aside all that is merely the clothing and expression of sanctity, and to find that the underlying substance is simply the love of God and of things Divine carried to an heroic degree; we cannot expect to gain much definite profit from the study of saints' lives. Nothing comes out more clearly in these pages than that the saints themselves have been careful to separate from the essence of sanctity those extraordinary gifts and "charismata" in which it is vulgarly sup-

PREFACE

posed to consist; and to place its whole inner substance in an eminent or heroic degree of that charity which is possessed by every soul in grace, and which St Paul sets above tongues, above prophetic insight or foresight, above miracles, even above martyrdom and self-sacrifice when they are not the fruits of charity.

What at once interests us and helps us, is the discernment of one and the same Spirit under a diversity of manifestations. In the saints of all ages and countries taken together the full content of the idea of Christian sanctity is unfolded to us. In them we see how that Spirit which found its fullest and most unimpeded expression in the life of the God-man and of His Blessed Mother, has also uttered itself in a thousand languages in the lives of His saints, the members of that mystical body which Christ rules and animates, as making with Himself the full organ of Divine manifestation. However differently it may act and be reacted on by its conditions and surroundings, charity is one and the same thing in the Head and in the members; in the perfect saint and in the beginner; in every nationality and climate; in every stage of civilisation or barbarism; in every condition of life, in high or low, rich or poor, old or young; in every variety of mind, character, temperament; whether it languish or flourish; whether it be the first or last smouldering spark, or else the living flame of heroic sanctity. Nor is this a mere oneness of type, or resemblance—a parallelism and similarity of spirit such as exists between the disciples of a master, or the copies of an original. For whatever may be disputed as to

PREFACE

the indwelling of one and the same God in the natural conscience of all men, binding them as to a common centre, it is the plain teaching of the Church that the Spirit which utters itself in the supernatural life of grace is not multiplied in the multitude of souls nor divided among them, but is identically one and the same in all.

In the measure then that we detect this "unity in variety" among the saints and learn to regard each several life as a self-revelation of that Divine personality with which they were in some sort 'possessed'; in the measure that we come to disregard the mere husk of language and to look to the hidden sense of that revelation, we shall learn that in our degree we too can lay hold of that same sense and give it utterance in a language all our own.

Not indeed that all are capable of sanctity, which is the heroism of charity, but that all can drink in some measure of the chalice which the saints have drained. It is by the interspersion of men of special and extraordinary gifts, graces, and abilities, that God makes provision for the many. He breaks and multiplies bread and gives it to his apostles to divide to the multitudes; and this law obtains even in the distribution of that grace which in some measure is needful for all. Still the difference here between greatest and least is one of degree, not of kind, and it would be to render the example of the saints wholly unfruitful were we to lose sight of this, and, by confounding the phenomena of sanctity with its substance, to regard it as belonging to an order of things in no way concerning us.

PREFACE

It is hoped that M. Joly's work may tend to dispel such an illusion wherever it exists, and prepare many minds to draw more abundant profit than heretofore from the contemplation of the " great cloud of witnesses " by which we are encompassed.

G. T.

LONDON, *May* 7, 1898.

CONTENTS

CHAPTER I

THE IDEA OF SANCTITY IN THE DIFFERENT RELIGIONS   PAGE 1

The idea of sanctity—its history—the saint among the Chinese—among the Buddhists—among the Mohammedans—in the Old Testament—in the New—among the principal Christian denominations—the saint in the Catholic Church—the "great man" and the saint—points of affinity and divergence—greater unity, more liberty, more unlimited progress in the saint—the saints and their surroundings—the saint and the mystic—all mystics not saints—are all saints mystics?—false definitions of mysticism—true definition—mysticism is the love of God—the saint, a man who serves God in an heroic manner and from the motive of love.

CHAPTER II

HUMAN NATURE IN THE SAINT   42

Sanctity and natural gifts—saints, by nature, neither half-witted nor of weak constitution—diversities of character among the saints—how far these extend—they show themselves in great things and in small—meaning of this latter word as applied to saints—humour in saints—tastes and personal habits.

CONTENTS

CHAPTER III

EXTRAORDINARY PHENOMENA IN THE LIVES OF
THE SAINTS   64

Extraordinary states and states of ill health in the saints
—is sanctity a nervous disease?—its relation to certain
recently discussed phenomena of mental-hearing, second
sight, and clairvoyance—the nature of these phenomena in
the saints—revelations, visions, prophecies: they do not
constitute sanctity, but the sanctity of the person gives
them credibility and value—testimony of St John of the
Cross—St Theresa—St Jane de Chantal—teaching of
Benedict XIV.—this applies also to miracles—three kinds
of ecstasy—how the saints, taught by experience, have
distinguished between them — so-called hysteria in the
saints—Père Hahn and M. Janet—accidental phenomena
overcome or transformed—in the saints there is no disintegration, narrowness or dual personality, but an evolution of an absolutely different kind.

CHAPTER IV

THE SENSES AND IMAGINATION—THE INTELLECT
AND CONTEMPLATION   118

Theoretic psychology of the saints—the help they derive from
the senses—the pre-eminent position they accord to the will,
when guided by love—does the saint materialise his conceptions or does spirituality gain the ascendency over him?—
distinction he draws between the eternal essence of God and
God made man in the person of our Lord—error of the
quietists—how the imagination, as soon as it has been purified, becomes once more free—theory of St John of the
Cross—what the saint chiefly requires of the intellect is that
it should begin to love—reflection and doubt—the sceptic
and the believer—the heretic and the saint—what the intellect of the saint desires and obtains by means of prayer—self-

CONTENTS

scrutiny in the saint—experiences of St Chantal—Bossuet's principles—the saint's knowledge of his own sanctity—contemplation or so-called passive prayer—the effect and cause of steady and fruitful labour — accumulated piety and reflection.

CHAPTER V

FEELING, LOVE AND ACTION 148

Feeling in the saints—how much of it is due to their physical organisation and extent to which this latter is modified in them—predominant part taken by the heart—notable examples—the saint's aptitude for suffering and emotion—by what things is he moved?—his feelings are like ours, only that he has got rid of self-love—human and natural affections—supernatural and heavenly affections—friendship and innocent pleasures—the love of God in the saints—its connection with suffering which is accepted, sought and asked for—its connection with action—how the saint's capacity for action is fostered by his love of suffering, by his method of contemplation, and by the purity of his faith—joy in suffering—spiritual child-bearing—the great precept of St Ignatius regarding resolutions made in times of consolation—the active life of the saints—how they carry it out—conclusion.

THE PSYCHOLOGY OF THE SAINTS

CHAPTER I

THE IDEA OF SANCTITY IN THE DIFFERENT RELIGIONS

IF unenlightened piety has frequently changed and distorted the features of the saints, the dilettantism of more than one neo-Christian of the present day promises to be no less destructive in its effects. Raised far above the level of human nature, the saints seemed, as it were, altogether outside of it, and as Mgr. Dupanloup remarks so forcibly, one had almost begun to question whether "they were really men, sons of Adam, with flesh and blood like our own." The inclination nowadays is, on the contrary, to explain everything in them as due to natural and social influences, of a kind to which any one of us might be exposed. They are set down, many of them, as morbid, hysterical, hypnotic persons, who, by reason of the innate or acquired delicacy of their nervous systems, were endowed with second sight, like these well-known somnambulists who have been restored to health by the marvellous and well-attested power of hypnotism. Or else, according to the fashion of the day, the life of some saint is taken up for the purpose of obtaining a better understanding of some period in the history of art or popular literature. Unexpected discoveries are made and, though naturally surprised, the student is overjoyed. He had thought that he was only dealing with a saint, and lo and behold, he meets a man or a woman, as the case may be. He gives an account of his discovery to his circle of readers in the tone of one who half expects to be set down in consequence as a lover of paradoxes, but who, as a sensible man, is able to face that prospect with tolerable equanimity. If he finds that his subject was more solicitous of the spirit than of the letter, that he was not narrow-minded but possessed a good deal of initiative, tenderness, respect for conscience, a love of the beautiful and even some regard for cleanliness, he thinks that he has chanced upon a rare case. He treats this unexpected self-assertion on the part of outraged nature as an instance of retrogression or atavism or else he credits heresy with one more precursor or unconscious disciple.

We have no need to complain of these many fanciful theories. Some of them are very artistic and there is at least this much to be said for them all, that they are a proof that not only literature, but science and psychology would find the saints an interesting subject of study.

Not an easy one though, by any means, but that is only an extra reason for undertaking it.

More than one simple and conservative soul has been annoyed by the way in which a certain distinguished priest, a member of the Institute of

THE IDEA OF SANCTITY IN RELIGIONS 3

France and Director of the Ecole Française in Rome, has handled the legends of the saints. I need hardly say that he has shewn no want of reverence in his treatment of them. After all, we are not afraid of clearing away the *bric-à-brac* which accumulates in course of time and disfigures our ancient cathedrals. It is a measure of necessity if they are ever to regain their primitive beauty and purity of style. What is there to prevent our doing in the case of psychology what we naturally do in the case of history and architecture? I am not, of course, advocating restorations and reconstructions, after the fashion of certain modern artists who, indirectly, attempt to credit past generations with ideas which never entered their heads. But there is more than one saint to whom "restitution" is due, and the work is one of devotion no less than of good taste. If there are men who have nothing to lose and everything to gain from the simple truth, surely these men are the saints.

It will be useful if, before entering upon a closer study of the saints themselves, we ask what signification the word Saint has borne in different languages. The idea of sanctity is nothing new, but men's conception of it has varied. To write its history and to endeavour to discover how it has been looked upon in this or that centre of civilisation is to attempt to take the measure of the most sublime —or the most ambitious—of all the aspirations that have ever characterised the human race.

To go back to the very beginning of things.

Christianity has "reformed" nature and we believe that in doing so it has fortified and set it free as well. But the same God who redeemed nature, had also, in the first instance, created it and, to borrow the words of the liturgy, created it "admirably." Mankind, in the interval, had made attempts, many and great and with very unequal success, to rise to the height of great virtue. Did they ever attain to sanctity? They certainly desired it and even made profession of it, and thus, in some little way, enjoyed a foretaste of it.

To get even as far as this it was first necessary that they should rise out of the savage state of the so-called primitive races. So long as poor humanity made the most of its relationship to the inferior creation—animals, plants, wind, sun; so long as the courage or strength of a man was considered to depend upon his power of appropriating to himself the nature of a buffalo, a bear or a shark, by eating them or taking their name; so long as rain-makers, wizards and chiefs derived their power from strange alliances with the elements or animals, man's ambition was to become more material rather than more pure-minded and more spiritual. The faint traces of religion found in the legends handed down in his tribe could not help him; as in mythology—in spite of the endless variety of its forms—"spirits" were generally represented as malevolent and wicked. Before the idea of sanctity can dawn upon him, man's intelligence has to advance so far that he can desire, hope and seek for a means of freeing himself from his misery. He must be stirred and attracted by the idea of a higher sort of existence. At the very least, he must be able to despise the gross pleasures and degrading fears that excite and oppress the majority of his fellows.

The Chinese are supposed, and not without reason, to be a people little given to ideals and therefore unable to understand a kingdom that is not of this world—but their philosophers very early began to make distinctions between different levels in human nature. Above the ordinary man, they placed the wise man who respects and cultivates his own reason and strives incessantly to put in practice the known principles of a virtuous life and, if he can, to discover fresh ones. Above the wise man, they place the saint or perfect man, who lives "like the spirits" and practises, this time without effort, calmly and tranquilly, the law of heaven, which is perfection and truth unmixed with any alloy.[1] We are not told the origin of this law, or mandate from heaven, as it is called, in one of their sacred books,[2] or from what source those who practise it derive the strength necessary to them. When the metaphysical problem comes to the fore, the learned Chinaman holds his peace. Those who pretend to have discovered his secret thoughts on the subject, say that he holds sanctity to be the product of heredity, which is only avoiding the difficulty.

Instead of expecting the Chinese to tell us, what

[1] A former missionary, M. l'abbé Coldre, who spent fifteen years in China, tells me that what struck him as the dominant idea in this conception (of sanctity) was the idea of *absolute rectitude.*

[2] See De Lanessan, *La morale des philosophes chinois*, Paris, 1896.

they have never been at the pains to find out, we will content ourselves with noting that in their eyes, sanctity is the most perfect state of human nature; that to attain to it is a law of our being, and lastly, that this law establishes a fundamental opposition between the earth and what—without explaining or defining it—their writers call Heaven.

But if the divine action is only very dimly recognised in the Chinese conception of sanctity, it is otherwise in the Greek.

It is a remarkable fact that with the Greeks, virtue was held to be the result of purely human activity, while sanctity was associated with the idea of a nearer and more intimate approach to the Divinity. We possess a dialogue on sanctity by Plato entitled *Euthyphro*.[1] It treats exclusively of the question, "Is sanctity sanctity because it is pleasing to the gods, or is it pleasing to the gods because it is sanctity?" Plato naturally inclines to this latter solution. He wishes to prove that all virtue is such as it is, by reason of its own essence which is eternal and immutable, and that if this essence is, in reality, one with the supreme good which is God, it cannot be dependent upon the arbitrary will of any capricious divinity. Plato does not, however, define sanctity. He will do so, he says, "on another occasion,"—his favourite method of disposing of delicate questions. However, the idea of sanctity and the idea of what is specially pleasing to the Divinity are evidently closely connected in his mind.

[1] See Appendix.

The word sanctity was evidently familiar to more thoughtful minds, for we even find it in Epicurus. Cicero is our informant.[1] "Epicurus had written books upon sanctity and piety towards the gods." Cicero adds, it is true, "The man is laughing at us here" (*ludimur ab homine*), because, according to Cicero, it was impossible to speak seriously of sanctity and piety towards the gods and at the same time to believe that everything is caused by the chance bringing together of certain atoms, and that in man, truth, happiness and virtue come from the senses. Still, this is another instance of the association between the idea of sanctity and the idea of piety towards the gods and it is worthy of notice.

Of all religions (other than our own) Buddhism is the one which has most insisted upon the necessity of sanctity. Here, however, the idea that the saint is a being who is pleasing to God and who serves Him better than other men, has completely disappeared. The Buddhist saint thinks he is holy because he has suppressed or annihilated nature, but he stops at this and does not advance to union with a God who communicates to him a share in His own virtue. The gods themselves he looks upon as beings who are products of the unlimited metamorphoses of a nature which is not only eternal but eternally bad. These gods and the heaven they inhabit belong to this detested world—all the more so, as a being who has once been a god may afterwards become a horse or some other animal. They do, indeed, possess a hierarchy amongst themselves,

[1] Cicero. On the Nature of the Gods. II, 41.

and some have a higher place in it than others, but the highest class still suffer from certain remains of terrestrial impurity which separates them from the goal they are bound to desire equally with man, and that goal is Nirvana!

In attaining to it, the gods are of no assistance to man. He has to discover for himself, how to escape that purposeless series of alternative births and deaths from which the god himself, as soon as he begins to exist, is not exempted. He has to save himself, to deliver himself and to sanctify himself. To the Buddhist these three expressions are synonymous. In his eyes, sanctity is deliverance and deliverance is the extinction of evil as well as the end of all things, since everything is evil: it is Nirvana.

More than one philosopher has been puzzled at the sight of a religion without God and at this aspiration towards nothingness, and has suggested that this nothingness means rest in the plenitude of a henceforth immutable existence, but there is no Hindu text to tell us so. The most that can be said is that no Hindu text denies it expressly, but what is much more certain is that it is a question to which Buddha did not, of set purpose, wish to give any answer.[1] He held the care of escaping from these perpetual reincarnations to be of such importance that it

[1] See Oldenberg's recent standard work (French translation): "*Bouddha—sa vie—sa doctrine—sa communauté.*" The quotations I shall presently give, are taken from this work. Those who still wish to deny the existence of such an individual as Buddha, may substitute in his stead the school of thinkers who originated and propagated his doctrine. It will serve equally well for the purposes of my comparison.

ought to outweigh all others. This is very clear from the following curious text. "Does or does not the perfect man live after death? The Sublime Buddha has taught nothing on this subject. He has not revealed it. Because this knowledge would not assist the saint or help to a pious life, to detachment from earthly things, to cessation, to repose, to knowledge, to illumination, to Nirvana, therefore the Sublime One has not revealed it."

What he did reveal to his followers on every occasion was the necessity of annihilating in themselves every desire and of renouncing all action, because action and desire are but one and the same thing at bottom. "The nature of man depends upon his desires. Such as his desire, so is his will, so are his works, so is the existence which falls to his lot." As all existence is pain, the way of salvation lies in suspension of all desire. This suspension will not, at once, kill the present life, but what is far better, it destroys the germs of future lives, and so the object of existence is attained. The faithful, therefore, have carefully retained and meditated upon these words of Buddha. "Whilst I gave myself up to these contemplations, my soul was delivered from the sin of covetousness, the sin of attachment to earthly things, the sin of error, the sin of ignorance. A consciousness of deliverance is evoked in the one who is delivered; the necessity of rebirth is done away with, sanctity is attained, duty is fulfilled; I shall return no more to this world." This world is the world in which the gods are, as well as men, since Buddha had been a god.

It is easy to see how superficial minds and those whose object it is to cast discredit upon Christianity have been, in this instance, led astray. The Buddhist monk and the Buddhist "saint" have often been compared to the Christian monk and saint. The reason given is that when the Buddhist wants to be a saint, he must begin by becoming a monk, and the Indian monk is obliged to renounce domestic and family life, to profess absolute poverty and continency, to beg his bread, to practise passive contemplation and, if he possibly can, to be wrapt in ecstasy. But his motive for despising the flesh and everything connected with it, is not because it is subject to corruption and death, but because it is subject to indefinite existence. His object is not, therefore, to reform the world and to introduce fresh life into it by unfolding new forms of activity. He desires to cut himself off completely from the world, both present and future. The Buddhist saint renounces all action as well as all desire in order to deliver himself from the obligation of being born again. In his eyes, this deliverance is sanctity, and sanctity itself is neither more nor less than this deliverance.

It would be hard to find a greater contrast than exists between the Buddhist fundamental conception of sanctity and the Mahomedan. I say fundamental, because, to judge from appearances one might easily imagine that the Buddhist monk and Mussulman marabout resemble one another pretty closely. Both renounce the world, both seek solitude and retirement, both practise long vigils, fasting and abstinence, both aspire to visions and ecstasy and both would have us believe that they attain to them. But if the former aims at the suppression of existences, the latter desires a rebirth, for all eternity, of his bodily faculties, and if he renounces a certain number of pleasures in this life it is in the hope of enjoying many more in the world to come. While the former does without gods, the latter aspires to intercourse with the god he invokes. In India, the word saint means "one who is delivered," in Islamism the name "marabout," which is given to a man who is already prepared for sanctity or who is instructed in the way of it, signifies "one who is tied or bound." Tied or bound to whom? To God, for the saint or *ouali* is, properly speaking, the friend of God. "The marabout who has attained to this degree of perfection (ecstasy) is called *ouali*, the friend of God, a saint. He is worshipped by the faithful, and after his death they profess themselves his religious servants. It is orthodox, under these conditions, to implore his intercession by means of prayer, with God and his prophet.[1]

If we ask, by what means the fact of this intercession, which is the fruit or reward of sanctity is revealed, the Mussulman answers: by countless miracles. He has the less difficulty in enumerating them as on the one hand, he holds every natural phenomenon, which is not foreseen and expected, habitual and of daily occurrence, to be miraculous; and on the other, as no clergy has ever been at

[1] Colonel Trumelet. "The Saints of Islam," introd. xix.

the pains to verify these legends of the "saints" for him, he accepts everything, even such stories as those of mountains sinking into the earth and the moon being cut in half.

Despite his fasts and his miracles, the saint of Islam is not unmindful of self, nor has his prophet been unmindful of him in dispensing the joys of his paradise. "This singular hagiography," says a commentator,[1] "reveals the object or determining cause of miracles to be, in the case of the Mussulman, to a great degree tainted by the materialism inherent in Mahomedanism. The private interests of the saint are too frequently set before those of the divinity who has bestowed upon him a share in his power. In other words, the saint of Islam too often uses his gifts for his own purposes and for the gratification of his passions."

These first considerations shew us that, above rectitude and honesty, above wisdom and talent and intellectual greatness, mankind very early conceived the idea of a still more perfect mode of existence. All nations were not able to understand that this perfection could only be the fruit of intercourse with a god, some absolutely denied that it could be so, but the majority felt instinctively that such heights were unattainable to human nature without the assistance of an attraction and strength that could only come from a divine source. It was to this explanation of the "mandate from heaven" that all, even the Chinese, inclined, when they tried to find out what was really involved in the idea of sanctity.

[1] *Id., ibid.*, lviii.

THE IDEA OF SANCTITY IN RELIGIONS

It is, above all, among the Hebrew people and in the Bible that we find the idea of sanctity most intimately associated with the idea of God. In Exodus, Leviticus, Deuteronomy, God alone is holy. If He communicates a share of His holiness to one of His creatures, He does so, in virtue of a special decree of His Providence, as a mark of special favour, guaranteed by a visible consecration. It is also a free gift, bestowed, in the first instance, independently of any human merit. It can be conferred upon inanimate objects. There are sacred places, sacred days, sacred unctions, sacred vestments, sacred victims and sacred meats.

"Thou shalt make," says the Book of Exodus, "also a plate of the purest gold, whereon thou shalt grave with engraver's work: Holy to the Lord. And thou shalt tie it with a violet fillet and it shall be upon the mitre... And the plate shall be always on his (Aaron's) forehead, that the Lord may be well pleased with them."[1] The priests are holy, for they, as well as the victims they are to offer up, are consecrated to the Lord. "Neither shall they shave their head nor their beard.. for they offer the burnt offering of the Lord and the bread of their God and therefore they shall be holy."[2]

As a nation Israel is holy, not on account of the magnitude of its virtues or of its superabundant merits, but because God has chosen it and set it apart for His service. It is written in Leviticus: "You shall be holy unto me, because I the Lord am holy and I have separated you from other people,

---

[1] Ex. xxviii. 36, 37, 38.   [2] Lev. xxi. 5-6.

that you should be mine."[1] And in Deuteronomy, "Thou art a holy people to the Lord thy God."[2]

Even in the Old Testament, however, we find a gradual development of ideas. At first, sanctity was connected chiefly with ceremonial, it consisted in an absolute fidelity to material and carnal rites. Slowly but surely, the Divine action began to penetrate from exterior things to interior. Even in the books quoted above, the man who had been purified and consecrated to the Lord is urged to conform himself, as far as he can, to the likeness of the God who has elected him. "Let them therefore be holy, because I also am holy, the Lord who sanctify them" (Lev. xxi. 8), and "He will keep the feet of his saints, and the wicked shall be silent as darkness" (1 Kings ii. 9).

But in the Book of Kings, the purely moral conception of sanctity becomes gradually more prominent, although it still remains closely allied with the idea of God and His service. It is thrown into even stronger relief by a contrast of ideas altogether new in form: "With the holy one Thou wilt be holy, and with the valiant, perfect. With the elect Thou wilt be elect and with the perverse Thou wilt be perverse" (2 Kings xxii. 26). So also David in one of his Psalms (Ps. xvii. 26). He is in his turn called "the servant of the Lord," an expression sanctioned by God Himself, who speaks of "My servant Job." The latter is described, further on, in the Book of Tobias, as "the holy man Job." Not long afterwards, Elias is declared to be a man

[1] Lev. xx. 26.   [2] Deut. vii. 6.

of God, and of Eliseus it is said: "I know that this man is a man of God and holy."

What then, we may ask, is, in future, to be the distinguishing mark between the saint or man of God, and the impious and ungodly? Not outward ceremonial and fidelity in offering sacrifices, as we learn from the example of Job and the teaching of those who, in sacred writ, are always recalling to our minds the virtues of the "holy patriarchs." The prophets, witness Isaiah and Jeremiah, are energetic in their declarations that purity of heart is of more avail than purification by the blood of goats and heifers.

From the comparisons instituted above, we see that it is in the religion which ignores God that sanctity bears the most severe and repulsive aspect. To prejudiced minds, this may sound paradoxical. In point of fact, however, when God is got rid of, human nature is not emancipated. It becomes the hopeless slave of a fatalism, which, besides being utterly unintelligible, leads, as far as anyone can see, absolutely nowhere. All said and done, therefore, it is a moving sight, and one that does honour to our degenerate nature, to witness the despairing efforts of so many millions of men to escape from the bondage of the flesh. They have experienced to the full its bitterness and emptiness. The Mussulman believes and hopes in God, but then he expects to receive, in return, benefits calculated to make sanctity singularly attractive to those who have only outwardly renounced the pride of life and the lusts of the flesh. The Old Testament believer, on his side, at first submitted to a God who reserved sanctity for Himself alone and only demanded exact obedience, in return for which He promised earthly happiness. It was only very gradually that the man "who walked in God's ways" was led to aspire to being more than His servant. His heart, by degrees, became capable of higher, nobler sentiments. He realised at last, what all men require to know, that love is the only adequate return for love, both here and hereafter. This truth was in the mind of the author of the Book of Tobias when he wrote of the young couple in it: "They continued in good life and in holy conversation so that they were acceptable to both God and man" (Tobias xiv. 17).

We now come to the New Testament. Its followers are, it is true, divided among themselves, but on no subject have there been more lively discussions between them than on that of the cultus of the saints and their intercession, for they one and all believe in sanctity. From St Paul to St Francis of Assisi down to the very eve of the Reformation, there have been saints who are recognised by the Protestants of the present day, no less than by Catholics, as worthy of honour and imitation.

There is one point of even greater importance, upon which Catholics, as well as all Protestants who hold any kind of definite belief, are agreed. God is sanctity itself according to the Bible, but this sanctity is revealed to us in a more accessible form, for our imitation and guidance, in the person of Jesus Christ. In all their great works, published during the last twenty years, Protestants have taught that "the idea of sanctity was realised for the first time on earth in the person of Jesus Christ. Since His coming, we have not only known, but we have witnessed what real sanctity is like in this world."

These same Protestant theologians are careful to point out, what, in their opinion, is the difference between the just man and the saint. The just man or man who has been justified, obeys the precept of Jesus Christ when He said, "Come to Me." The saint or man who has been sanctified, goes one step further. He answers to the invitation which says "Abide in Me and I will abide in thee." When all due allowance has been made for the infinite variety of opinion existing among the Protestant sects, we may be allowed to select the following from among their formularies. "Sanctification demands good works proceeding from regeneration of heart, by means of faith." Faith, that is to say, in the Divinity of Christ, faith in the possibility of becoming a participator in His Divinity, who has vouchsafed to become a participator in our humanity.[1]

Having established so much common ground

---

[1] See "Encyclopédie Religieuse." Paris: Fischbauer. 1889. Art.: Saint and Sanctity. We must confess that these ideas are very different from those held by Luther, and that, at any rate, the most extreme and sectarian of his views are passed over in silence. In Luther's opinion, Christian sanctity was only an *imputed* sanctity which did not essentially change us, but only threw the cloak of Christ's merits over the perversities of our nature. These merits were imputed to us by faith, without the necessity of good works on our part.

between us, we will go on to consider, what chiefly interests us, namely, the saints of the Catholic Church. Controversy apart, all who really wish to study sanctity from the point of view of psychology, and in order to sound the innermost depths of the human soul, acknowledge that by "saints" we mean the saints who have been verified, proclaimed, honoured and written about by the Catholic Church. These are the real saints in the eyes of the literary man and the psychologist, no less than of the public at large. It will not be unprofitable to consider in what way, by what means, at what cost and with what profit to themselves, these extraordinary beings so far outstripped the ordinary run of their fellow-creatures.

This relationship of the saints to Jesus Christ has been fully explained to us by that Apostle, who, in mind, bore the closest resemblance to Him, for he was the most apostolic of all the Apostles. Protestants acknowledge that it was necessary that God should reveal His sanctity to us in the person of Jesus Christ. Why should it not be expedient that the sanctity of Jesus Christ should take a more human form still in the person of His nearest disciples and notably in the one of whom it has been said that "his heart was the very heart of Christ"? "Cor Pauli, cor Christi erat."[1] His Master had, indeed, taken our humanity upon Himself, but who can wonder, if a humanity united so intimately with

---

[1] St John Chrysostom. Abbé Fouard has inscribed these words at the head of one of the chapters in his interesting book on St Paul. (Paris: Lecoffre.)

the Divine essence, still appeared too far above our reach? In the sanctity of the Apostle, we find the heart of Christ united this time with moral and not only bodily infirmity. He has still to struggle against the sinful inclinations of his nature, and in spite of his marvellous conversion, he is still liable to all the temptations and subject to all the miseries of our fallen race.

It is worth while to pause and consider for awhile his striking personality. Many people know no more of the Apostle than they learn from those portions of his Epistles which are read in church. On these solemn occasions, they speak to us in the name of the Universal Church, uniting both Old and New Testaments and so interpreting the mysteries of both laws. But what is naturally calculated to increase the respect entertained for them by the faithful tends somewhat to obscure their historical value for those who never read them at any other time.

We have only to turn to the Epistles themselves, however, to hear the very tones of the man who gathered the tradition concerning Jesus Christ from eye-witnesses and who himself saw Him in vision. The historical events in which he took part establish a visible link between his preaching and that of Christ Himself, and, read in connection with them, the most dogmatic texts are invested with a human and personal meaning without losing anything of the majesty attaching to revealed truths.

Read in the light of their own times and of their own social and geographical surroundings, the Epistles recall still more vividly the human personality of their author. All his sufferings, his anguish, his struggles, alternating with the inspirations of grace, are made known to us. Heedless of the dangers which encompass him, the most sublime doctrines burst from his lips in the unstudied and familiar language of burning zeal, with now and again a certain reticence due to the demands of human prudence. The saying "*Foris pugnae, intus timores,*" which he seems to have adopted for his own, may very well stand, in future, as the motto for all the saints. To enemies, he exhibits a martyr's courage; to friends, superiors and equals alike, he reveals his interior sufferings, his temptations, and his trials of faith. To the rest of the disciples, he shews himself in a more subdued light. To them, he appears less eager indeed for the fight, but also less weighed down with sorrows, for he fears to discourage weak and timid souls. St Paul is therefore the great Apostle of the sanctity of the New Dispensation, no less than of its dogma.

His leading idea is that Christ, in dying for men, invited all to live a new life in Him, a life of sanctity. He often calls those of the faithful who had known Jesus Christ when he was on earth, by the name of saints, and later on he gives the same title to those who, in the midst of a pagan society, renounced its superstitions and lived a life apart and among themselves for the sake of more carefully preserving the deposit of faith. In St Jerome's time the word still bore this same signification. Strictly speaking, the Christian life and the life of sanctity should be synonymous terms, for the Catholic Church has never ceased to remind us that we are all called to be saints. But did St Paul mean that everyone who renounced paganism and believed in Jesus Christ, had thereby attained to perfect sanctity? Surely not, since he recognises not only different ministries and offices, a diversity of spiritual gifts and unequal graces in the Church of God, but likewise many degrees in that charity which is to be preferred to the Apostleship or the gifts of prophecy and miracles. To a select few, who had carried their detachment from the things of this world to its utmost limits, far more than to the ordinary run, the *turba magna*, of the elect, he applied these words: "For whom He foreknew He also predestinated to be made conformable to the image of His Son, that he might be the first-born amongst many brethren" (Rom. viii. 29).

Were these brethren content to dwell in peace in the bosom of this holy family? Had they nothing further to do except to keep themselves pure and to abstain from anything that would render them unworthy of their vocation? Were they the servants of God and nothing more? The great Apostle, who trod so closely in the footsteps of the "First Born," has described sanctity to us in these astounding words: "I fill up what was wanting in the sufferings of Christ."[1] Bossuet interprets these words to mean that Christ only suffered in Jerusalem and that it was necessary that the cross should be carried to Rome and Greece and from thence to all parts of

[1] Coloss. i. 24.

the world.[1] A deeper meaning is given to them by one who was Bossuet's contemporary and inferior to him as a writer, but who approached nearer to sanctity certainly than he did, since the process of his canonisation has already begun. I mean M. Olier, the founder of St Sulpice. "The feast of All Saints," he says, "appears to me, in some sort, a greater feast than that of Easter or the Ascension. Our Lord is made perfect in this mystery, because, as our Head, He is only perfect and fulfilled when He is united to all His members, the saints."[2] And again, "This feast is glorious, because it manifests exteriorly, the hidden life of Jesus Christ. The greatness and perfection of the saints is entirely the work of His spirit dwelling in them."

This participation in the spirit of Jesus Christ is rightly the destiny of each one of the faithful. Few, however, attain to it in a high degree, and it is to the few who do, that the Church, properly speaking, reserves the name of saints.

If, therefore, we have rightly interpreted the beautiful words of M. Olier, the saints are destined to manifest exteriorly the "hidden" life of our Lord, but in order to do this, they must have begun by "hiding" Him in their hearts. This was what was said of St Francis of Assisi by his celebrated "three companions" who wrote his life. They applied St Paul's words to him: "*Studebat in interiorem hominem recondere Jesum Christum.*" He strove to hide Christ within his heart. These

---

[1] See the *Panégyrique de S. Paul.*
[2] Letters, II., p. 475 (Lecoffre).

two ideas are not mutually antagonistic, as we shall see more fully later on. When the interior is filled with the spirit of Christ, exterior action flows from it, as from its true source and, sometimes in one direction, sometimes in another, fertilises the field of this world's activities, for the benefit of mankind.

All this is likely enough to provoke the scepticism of those who persist in regarding the saint as a man who despises nature and society. It will in no way surprise those who are accustomed to recognise the handiwork and influence of the saints in the evolutions and revolutions through which the human race has passed. The saint, although he is a man of God, is still a man, and a man who has not developed and raised himself under the influence of grace, in the direction of the supernatural and eternity alone. Bossuet[1] calls the saints "Those great men who planted the Church of God." It will be of interest to determine in what they resemble and in what they differ from the men who have been great in the purely human and profane sense of the word.

We will not waste time over the too easy task of instituting a comparison between the virtues which have raised men of the humblest capacities to greatness, and the weaknesses which, in other men, have not prevented them from reaching eminence in the sphere of art or science.

Which of these two kinds of greatness is least out of reach of the immense majority of men? Many will say that nothing in this world is more difficult than sanctity, and to judge from the obstacles which

[1] See sermon for the feast of All Saints.

our own imagination places in the way of it, they would seem to be right. But the wish, in this case, may be father to the thought. Our own sensuality makes us willing to find excuses and even justification for our weakness. And yet, as we have just seen, the doctrine that we are all of us called to sanctity is one of the principal truths of Christianity. Genius needs preparation, circumstances, exceptional materials, forerunners, a field of action favourable to its development, an innate appreciation of the needs of the times. It demands, as it were, its theatre and admiring crowds, the adjuncts of worldly power, glory and reputation. These things have, I know, fallen to the lot of some saints who have been intrusted with the government or defence of the Church and who have had, in consequence, to take part in the struggles and victories of civilisation. But how many more have been content to be salt of the earth, and to teach men by their example to esteem the lowliest duties and the most despised vocations. To say that any man can be great no matter what his condition may be, is an absurd contradiction in terms, but there have been saints in every conceivable state of life.

If we take account of those professions which were abandoned at the moment of conversion after having been practised for long years before, we find comedians and a great many courtesans on the list of saints. As for these professions which saints, men and women, have continued to exercise, we find that the Church has not only canonised monks, side by side with dukes, duchesses, kings, queens, emperors

THE IDEA OF SANCTITY IN RELIGIONS

and empresses, but also merchants, school-masters, gardeners, workmen, shepherds and shepherdesses, lawyers, doctors, publicans, a retired public executioner, jailors, treasurers, magistrates, beggars, domestic servants, artisans, shoemakers, carpenters, blacksmiths, and fishermen!

"For the canonisation of a servant of God," says Benedict XIV., "it is sufficient that there be proof that he has practised those virtues which occasion demanded, in an eminent and heroic degree, according to his condition in life, rank and circumstances."

The Church stipulates, however, that this heroism should not have been the impulse of a moment, but that it should have been manifested all through life by means of varied and frequent acts. In the case of martyrs she is content with the witness afforded by their death, but this is because she holds the sacrifice of their lives they offer for the faith to be the summing up, as it were, of the heroism of their lives, both past and also future, had they been prolonged on this earth. This is also the teaching of Benedict XIV.[1]

---

[1] Benedict XIV. "On the Beatification and Canonisation of Saints," iii. 21.

As I am quoting him for the first time, I may as well say here that his great work is not so much a collection of rules imposed by authority for the recognition of sanctity, as an experimental treatise on what has been gradually revealed to the doctors and rulers of the Church by the action of Christianity upon succeeding generations and by the spontaneous development of sanctity. It has therefore an historical and psychological as well as a dogmatic interest.

The interior life is, for this reason, always far more prominent in the saint than in the great man. There never was a saint who did not live a life of extraordinary prayer, of constant interior raising up of the heart to God, and who did not love meditation and solitude. The great man, on the other hand, is set upon obtaining public triumphs. It may be that these triumphs are of a nobler sort than those achieved by the ordinary run of men, but they, none the less, serve to entangle him in polemical and scholastic disputes and, above all, in political quarrels. He needs partisans to aid him in the accomplishment of his designs. He seeks to obtain public favour and to compel admiration. When this has been achieved, he rules the destinies of men, changes the convictions and modifies the tastes of a whole nation, but he rarely gets thus far without having flattered their passions and pandered to their lower nature in a manner that destroys the peace of the individual conscience and often the peace of nations. When the saint acts, and even when he acts with most vigour, he seeks, as far as he is personally concerned, to disappear from the eyes of men, to live ignored and despised, and his only desire is to disseminate among his fellow-men, by means of prayer and self-sacrifice, the peace of heart which he has laboured to obtain for himself.

Then again, though he may be great in the estimation of the multitude and of those who only witness the exterior results of his labours, the great man is often petty in the eyes of those who are nearest to him and who see the weaknesses of his character. There is a proverb which says that no man is a hero to his *valet de chambre*. But the saint is holiest of all in the eyes of those who live with him and who are the witnesses of his hidden virtues, his tenderness of heart, his power with God, and his secret influence over souls. It is their part oftenest to enlighten the ignorance and dissipate the prejudices of those who misjudge him.

As a necessary consequence of this, the saint has also more liberty than the great man.—What! more liberty with his love of the letter of the law, of self-discipline, of submission to that grace which has transformed and conquered him? Yet so it is, and we do not need theology to prove it to us. The most elementary pagan philosophy tells us in the words of Seneca that to obey God is true liberty: *Parere Deo libertas est.* It also teaches us that a rule, adopted of our own free will, does not annihilate, but on the contrary, strengthens and consolidates liberty and confers upon it all those benefits which had been anticipated from it. I do not myself believe that genius is a product of the Unconscious, and that the destiny of great men is decreed by a law inscribed by fate upon their temperaments, circumstances or surroundings.[1] But in spite of the heroism of mind which makes them turn these latter to such brilliant advantage, they are in many ways victims to their tyranny—victims, that is to say, to the tyranny of the senses, of the passions, of ambition, of the circumstances

[1] On this subject see my book *Psychologie des grands hommes*. 2nd edition. Paris: Hachette.

they have themselves created and which so often recoil on their makers, of insincere admiration, and to the tyranny, yet more galling and disastrous in its effects, of the false friends whose envy they have aroused. Where do we find a great man who has not had to suffer humiliation, torment and misery from the reiterated attacks of these enemies? I do not believe in the necessary and inevitable madness of great men any more than I believe that there is a fatality over their destiny. Still, if no genius has ever begun his career as a madman, not a few have so ended it, and this has never been the case with any one of the saints.

But illness, obstacles, trials, the opposition of friends as well as enemies, all these the saint has experienced, as well as the humiliations attendant on self-knowledge, but he is not dominated or held captive by them. They are the daily bread upon which his sanctity thrives. According to St Theresa, this is the bread with which the saint must eat his other sublime and dainty food. He does not wish to eat one without the other, and he himself testifies that this coarse bread nourishes and sustains the most solid parts of his spiritual being.

This unassailable liberty is the source of that unity which we find in the lives of the saints and which we do not find, at least in the same degree, in those of great men. The latter are possessed with a dominant idea, a great design, to the realisation of which they devote the major portion of their lives. Every man of genius bestows some new thing upon humanity at large, or at any rate upon his fellow-countrymen, whether it be a new method or style, or new solutions of old problems in science or war, and his unity consists in his identification in history with the fortunes of his triumphant discovery. But outside the sphere of this single dominating interest, we find incoherences, disorders and miseries enough in his life. This inferior side of his nature frequently ends by entirely eclipsing the other and by bringing about a premature decay of his faculties. Too often the life of the man of genius is but a tissue of failures, useless sacrifices and painful and sanguinary defeats.

Finally the saint and the great man are opposed in this, that the progress of the saint is uninterrupted and has no visible limits. I do not subscribe to the wonderful theories that have been advanced as to the precocity of great men. A great deal has been said about the suddenness of their vocations and the perfection to which their works have instantly attained. It has been suggested as an explanation of the rapid decline of some great men, that they obeyed a mysterious instinct which forsook and left them helpless, as soon as their work was done. There is only a very relative degree of truth in this theory. There have been great men who were very precocious, others who were less so, and some who were not precocious at all. There are very few of them whose lives do not afford instances of hard work and struggle as a condition of success. Progress does not seem to be a necessary law of their being or a law that knows no exceptions. Some have ended by failure due to the abuse of their health or their power. Alexander died of drink. Louis XIV. and Napoleon left France exhausted and mutilated. Corneille at last wrote such tragedies as Pertharites and Suréna. The tool of the great sculptor or the brush of the great painter at length falls from his hand, and the brain of Newton, after enduring untold strain, sinks into a condition of senile apathy.

The sanctity of the saint, on the contrary, as everyone knows, goes on increasing to the very last day of his life. Whatever may be thought of his miracles (and I am not discussing that question just now), they are most numerous when he is on his death-bed. He is greater on the day of his death than ever before. It is then that his sanctity and power are most conspicuous.

Points of divergency do not, however, destroy points of resemblance. Genius and sanctity have often been united in one man, and so they cannot be natural enemies one of the other. The genius of St Augustine, St Thomas, St Louis, St Gregory the Great and St Gregory VII., did no harm to their sanctity and vice versa. The combination is a rare one, no doubt, for the saint avoids, far more than he seeks, opportunities of exterior action and of influencing political events and persons. In his mode of action and development, however, he has certain points of affinity with great men which it will be useful to notice.

They are neither of them, in reality, isolated in the circles in which they move, whether literary, artistic or political, or, in the case of the saint, moral, religious or charitable. They are the chosen ones among their fellows, whose advent is as rare as it is unforeseen. There would seem to be centres peculiarly favourable to the production of holiness, and these have their human and historical aspects. At one time they are those groups of men who longed after the solitude of the desert as a means of escape from pagan immorality, far more than from pagan institutions and ideas. Such, again, were communities; and those bands of apostolic and pioneer monks; and such, too, were those localities which produced more than one bold aspirant to martyrdom; and the sincere and earnest spirits who felt so deeply the need of reform. In the days when pagan sensuality was rampant, the independence of woman had to be vindicated by the esteem and practice of voluntary chastity, and we find St Jerome and St Augustine repeatedly urging men to embrace monastic celibacy. Later on, when the clergy were corrupt and many kept concubines, a king and a queen reformed them by the wonderful example they gave of the most difficult form of continency.[1] We find saints who taught the love of detachment and poverty to barbarians addicted to pillage and usury; others who opened monasteries of monks devoted to agriculture in the midst of warlike barbarians, and monasteries of learned monks among wild and ignorant tribes. Later on, again, there were saints who founded religious orders bound to absolute obedience, in opposition to an age given over to the spirit of

[1] See the new Life of S. Hedwige. Paris: Bloud et Barral.

revolt, schism and private judgment. Others founded free schools for secular priests at a time when rank was the only necessary qualification for the highest episcopal dignities. We might extend the list, but it would take too long to make it complete.

Were these successive creations of the saints only temporary expedients to meet the danger which threatened one day and passed away the next? Hardly; for the enemies they had to fight were rarely short-lived, and their great institutions owe their continued existence to the restoration or more exact interpretation (whenever needed) of the saintly and productive spirit of their founder. Whenever one of the standing needs of humanity asserts itself with greater intensity than before, and the want of a remedy threatens danger to the community, then an individual arises, who, without destroying the established order of things, adds a fresh force to those which Christianity has already at its disposal. In purely human matters, the man of genius acts in a similar way for the benefit of his own times and posterity.

Finally, though no country has been denied the privilege of producing saints, some countries seem to have been allowed to take possession of the most illustrious among them for the purpose of enabling them to obtain a world-wide influence.

It has often been remarked that if French literature has been less spontaneous, natural, and popular than many another, it has on the other hand been characterised by a sort of strong selective attraction which draws into its orbit numberless imperfect begin-

THE IDEA OF SANCTITY IN RELIGIONS 33

nings, undeveloped talents, tendencies and movements from other literatures of various descriptions. And something analogous may be observed in relation to the saints.

"It is a curious fact," says M. Bougaud in his life of St Chantal, "that scarcely one of the religious orders developed and spread throughout the world until after it had taken root in French soil. St Benedict lived and died in Italy, but St Maurus hastened to establish himself in France. St Columban came from Ireland, St Bruno from the banks of the Rhine, St Norbert from Germany, St Dominic from Castille, St Thomas of Aquinas from Italy, St Ignatius from Pampeluna. They were all foreigners, urged by some mysterious influence to come to France, either because God, who had predestined her to be the eldest daughter of the Church, wished to give her the honour of a share in every great Catholic work, or else because the French genius, so full of brightness and vigour, is especially fitted to impress upon those works, those characteristics of simplicity, charm, nobility and greatness which attract all minds and win all hearts."

Then as to the times in which the saint lived. He has more apparent connection with the state of things which is the result of his action, than with that which immediately preceded his advent, and we may say the same of the great man. The latter has often a long battle to fight before his work, discovery or strategy is accepted by the world. The victory once gained, the distance between him and his fellow-countrymen or the world at large, disappears, and this is one of the signs that his work is really a creative one, and that he deserves to be ranked among great men. So it is with the saint. There never was an apostle, a founder of an order, an initiator of a new devotion destined to spread universally in the Church, or a reformer, who did not have to suffer, not only from enemies but from friends, his brethren in the faith.

All true greatness, whether in the way of genius or sanctity is, at first sight, a shock to lovers of mediocrity and routine. The man who demands effort and self-sacrifice from those who are reluctant to give either, naturally exposes himself to objections, suspicion, doubts and accusations brought sometimes in good faith and sometimes in bad. But once the time of trial is over, a new force is found to be within reach of souls. Eyes which sought a purer light, willingly follow it when it shines before them; hearts which were weighed down with a weariness they could not understand, eagerly answer to the call, and henceforward, weak souls find a path hewn out for them, where formerly there was none.

So then, we see that no matter how great the distance may be between nature and grace, between religious and social life, there is no necessary gulf between them. They may even be brought into close and very close connection with one another. Needless to say there is no antagonism between them. Those who think that there is, are deceived, partly because they confound sanctity too entirely with mysticism, but chiefly because they have a mistaken idea of what mysticism really is.

What then is Mysticism?

Philosophers have given us many definitions of it, and in particular Victor Cousin tells us that "it is the opposite of rationalism. It results from the despair of the intellect which has begun to doubt the power of reason and to dream of direct communication with God. It is a blind faith which strives to forget all the conditions to which our nature is subject, which will acknowledge no medium between God and man, either in the sensible universe or in reason, and which not only claims to see God face to face, but to unite itself to Him, sometimes through the feelings and sometimes through some other hidden agency. It forbids all reflection and condemns liberty, and in place of effort, substitutes contemplation, without thought and almost without consciousness."

We need hardly say that this kind of mysticism is not what Catholics and therefore certainly not what the saints mean by mysticism. It is true that they have no unbounded confidence in human reason. They believe that it was necessary that God should reveal certain truths which reason could not have discovered for itself. But it is one thing to recognise that reason has limits and another to condemn it as worthless and to regard all efforts made by it as useless. To say that Catholics refuse to recognise that nature is, in any way, a medium between God and man, is ridiculous.[1]

The mysticism of the saints is utterly different in kind from Alexandrian mysticism and the various other forms of mysticism to be met with in different philosophical systems.

After metaphysicians, come sociologists and moralists who tell us that mysticism is the opposite of naturalism. It condemns the earthly existence of man and has an equal contempt for society and nature. "The monk is the type of this frame of mind." He is without egotism, but also without individuality, family or country. He is full of charity for every description of misery but is himself an easy and docile prey "for despotism and superstition"![2] They give a satisfactory finishing touch to the description by adding "Mysticism is far older than Christianity. It is the real basis of Buddhism."

We have said enough already about the Buddhist idea of sanctity, to shew how artificial is this supposed likeness. Catholic mystics no more despise nature than they despise grace. All they say

[1] "It is necessary for us to understand that we ought to treat with suspicion anything which hinders us in such a manner as to take away our capacity for mental prayer, as we shall never in that way attain true spiritual liberty, one of the characteristics of that liberty being to enable us to find God in all things and to use creatures as a means of raising ourselves to Him."—St Theresa, Bk. of Foundations, ch. vi.

[2] See the philosophical leaflet of the *Journal des Débats* of Thursday evening, Aug. 8, 1895, Naturalism and Mysticism, by M. J. Bourdeau. (The author states that he is epitomising certain unpublished lectures of Taine's, which gives an added importance to his remarks.)

is that neither the one nor the other is self-sufficing and that by pretending to be so, they weaken and degrade themselves. It is a most arbitrary proceeding to insist upon attributing to the Catholic Church, an indifference and contempt which she has never, in any way, professed.

There are Christians, however, and even some Catholics, who believe that mysticism is the peculiar property of pure contemplatives, and that it destroys all interest in earthly things, all action properly so called, and anything like intellectual culture. They would be perfectly ready, therefore, to admit the truth of the following two-fold proposition. "All saints are not mystics and all mystics are not saints."

But is this proposition quite accurate? Certainly it is, if mysticism be what they define or imagine it to be; for all the saints did not live in the cloister, many were engaged in the business of this world, many founded schools of philosophy, many were married and bound by the deepest and tenderest ties of human love at the very time when the Church has decided that they were living a life of sanctity.

When I asked the opinion of one,[1] who has had a wide and varied experience of these matters, he replied emphatically: "No, all mystics are not saints." He declined, however, to agree to the first part of the proposition and he gave me the following definition of mysticism, the simplest and

---

[1] He will forgive me for mentioning his name—Abbé Huvelin. I am proud to be able to say that he and I were old companions at the Ecóle Normale.

clearest that I have ever come across. "Mysticism is the love of God."[1]

This definition, of course, requires to be amplified and developed, for the love we bear to God can never be an exact parallel to the love we bear to our fellow-creatures. It needs to be guided and enlightened. Plato's fable, according to which love is the offspring of wealth and poverty, has a certain amount of truth in it, for love gives and receives, but in very unequal proportions. The little child who loves its mother expects, and does in fact receive, everything from her. The God who loves His creatures with a Father's love, gives them everything they possess. In earthly loves, we each give and receive more or less, according to the richness and generosity of our nature. But when instead of giving his love to a fellow-creature, the mystic loves his God, however anxious he may be to carry His cross and share in His sufferings, he is still obliged to pray for and expect far more from God than he himself is able to give. The whole question is a delicate one and we shall have more to say upon it later on.

St Francis of Sales tells us very clearly that the love of God is the foundation and essence of Catholic mysticism. He says: Speculative theology tends to the knowledge of God. Mystical theology to the love of God   Mental prayer and mystical theology are one and the same thing   Mental prayer and mystical theology are neither more nor less than the loving intercourse which the soul holds

[1] V. Appendix.

with God, concerning His infinite goodness in uniting and joining Himself to her."[1]

When we come to reflect upon it, we see that every sort of love, no matter what its object may be, and in spite of absolute sincerity on the part of the lover, is subject to error, weaknesses and excess.

[1] Treatise on the love of God. IV. 1. Ed. of Annecy, p. 303.

It will be interesting to compare these definitions with the definitions given in dictionaries of the word mysticism.

The Academy dictionary says: "*Mystic*, one who refines in matters of devotion and the spiritual life; or (according to another definition in the same dictionary), of the interior life." The mystic is certainly devout and a lover of the interior and spiritual life. Nevertheless, the definition is a vague one, all the more so, as the word "refine" is one of those slightly disapproving, deceptive expressions, suggestive of a tendency, which is legitimate or not, according to the interpretation one chooses to put upon it.

Littré associates mysticism with the spiritual life, and defines the latter as: "Whatever has reference to the interior exercises of a soul freed from the senses, whose one desire is to perfect itself in the eyes of God." This definition is interesting and not inaccurate, but to readers of mystical books it will at once appear incomplete, if it is intended indirectly as a definition of mysticism as well. The definition in the *Encyclopédie des sciences religieuses* is equally unsatisfactory. It implies that mysticism is simply whatever is hidden from us in the actual conditions in which we are living, but which we feel to exist and towards which our soul naturally is attracted. Mysticism, according to this theory, is religion which supplements in each individual conscience, the "solid" but "limited" teaching of philosophy.

Each one of these explanations ignores the fact of the love of God, which, according to the best mystics, is the very soul itself of mysticism. If there is such a thing as a mystical knowledge, which is experimental and ineffable, it can be derived from nothing else but love. Gerson gives the following justly esteemed definition: "The subject-matter of mystical theology is an experimental knowledge of God which is the result of the embrace of unitive love." (Consider 28.)

It may be too exacting and jealous; it may demand more than its due and forget, in a measure, what it owes. Again, it may not recognise sufficiently the rights over it and the dignity of the object of its affections. These are dangers from which the love of God is not exempt. We gather this from the example of Fénelon and still more from the example of a multitude of souls less gifted and worse directed than he was.

True mysticism or love of God is, therefore, a first, and, it would seem, necessary step in the direction of holiness. It is but the first step, however, on a long and thorny path, along the whole of which frequent demands will be made upon body, mind and heart, in the way of effort and difficult undertakings.

Every Christian who is in a state of grace, loves God and is more or less of a mystic, but the mystic, properly so called, like the man whom we shall henceforward call "the saint," is one who is wrapped up in, and filled with, the love of God.

I have not the least intention of writing a dogmatic treatise on sanctity or of giving advice to those who wish to become saints. I shall have quite enough to do in endeavouring to point out what the soul of the saint possesses in common with us, and how these common attributes in his case develop and thrive. The saint, we know, is an heroic servant of God, a man who loves and is loved by God and who derives an extraordinary strength from this mutual love. Holiness, we know too, is not the annihilation, but the completion of our nature; for, as Spinoza says: "Man advances in perfection in proportion to the perfection of that object which he loves above all other things and which loves him in return."[1] It is not wrong to wish to know how, in the case of these favoured beings, sanctity transforms the faculties they share in common with those "whose miseries they have themselves experienced."

[1] Spinoza. Politico-theological treatise, chap. iv.

CHAPTER II

HUMAN NATURE IN THE SAINT

BEFORE enquiring what use sanctity makes of the natural gifts of the soul, it is of importance to ascertain whether sanctity "requires" the presence of any of these natural gifts, and, if so, of which. The word "requires" may appear somewhat too strong an expression under the circumstances, for many are inclined to leave a very wide field indeed to the mysterious operations of grace and the stirrings of the Spirit who breathes where He wills. Nevertheless, those who have really made a study of the lives of the saints, and whose duty it is to comment upon them, always take largely into account that foundation of natural character which sanctity transforms, but does not destroy.

No prudent ecclesiastical superior would admit to the priesthood, or the religious state, one whose mental organisation was defective.[1] St

---

[1] That is, defective in a way which would interfere with the attainment of the end of religious life. Fontenelle's well-known saying that Malebranche was of so weak a constitution that he was fitted, by nature and grace, for the ecclesiastical state, ought not to be pressed too far. Malebranche, as everyone knows, had an intellectual organisation which would have enabled him to shine anywhere as a philosopher and a writer.

John Chrysostom, in his magnificent treatise on the priesthood, long ago told us that, in order to exercise the sacred ministry, "a man must not only be pure, but he must also possess learning and experience." In like manner, solitude has great dangers, in the way of unwholesome dreaming, in store for weak, excitable souls, and those who find meditation a difficulty. A priest, one day, brought a penitent of his, of whose angelic piety he had a great opinion, to St Theresa. The saint was, all the same, extremely reluctant to admit her into the monastery. "You see, Father," she said, "even though our Lord should give this young girl devotion and teach her contemplation while with us, nevertheless, if she has no sense, she will never come to have any, and then, instead of being of use to the community, she will always be a burden." "An intelligent mind," she says again, "is simple and submissive; it sees its faults and allows itself to be guided. A mind that is deficient and narrow never sees its faults, even when shewn them. It is always pleased with itself, and never learns to do right."[1]

I have, therefore, no hesitation in admitting the truth of the following proposition, which is analogous to the one I discussed when speaking of mystics: All religious are not saints, and all saints are not religious. The life of sanctity differs from the

[1] Life of St Theresa according to the Bollandists. Paris: Retaux. II. 408. It is written by a Carmelite nun, and is one of the most delightful and solidly interesting books ever written by one woman of another.

religious life chiefly, it will be readily admitted, in that it surpasses it. From a purely human point of view, no one will deny that the Church has accomplished great things in the scientific no less than the social order. They may be open to criticism, but so are the achievements of politicians and the systems of metaphysicians. If the Church has left so deep an impression upon the secular history of mankind, if she has taught, civilised, conquered and organised so many countries and nations, it would be strange indeed if the saints, who are, as it were, her advance guard, had not had the chief share in all her good works. And yet, it is hard to believe that this extraordinary increase is all a gratuitous and miraculous gift from on high.

Joan of Arc has not suffered in her reputation either as a young girl or as a warrior, now that her sanctity has begun to attract general attention. She has lost none of the beauty, grace, wit, power of repartee and command of all the niceties of the French language, so much praised by Quicherat, Michelet and Sainte-Beuve; while her military genius, her knowledge of the tactics of war and the good use she made of the science of artillery, then in its infancy, are brought out in a work recently published by a French officer.

These various testimonies are summed up as follows, by an eminent psychologist of the Society of Jesus: "Joan of Arc is no blind and passive instrument of a supernatural power. An exterior intelligence does not take the place of her intelligence, or an exterior will of her will. The Deliverer of France is not a composite being, the dwelling-place, for the moment, of foreign powers. Joan knows that she possesses a very clearly defined personality of her own. She insists upon that fact, and she proves the truth of her claim by the independence of her decisions and actions, and by the resistance she occasionally offers to the guidance of her voices."

The above may be very properly applied to the majority of the saints,[1] and we may add in the words of the same Jesuit: "When God has some extraordinary mission in store for one of His creatures, He nearly always bestows natural gifts upon him which create in him a great aptitude for the work."

What Père de Bonniot says of Joan of Arc is obviously true of many great saints, from St Paul downwards. Still we ought not to dwell too much on this side of the question, nor must we forget what theologians tell us of the paradox and scandal of the cross, of these victories God wills to be gained by weakness in the natural order, by authority which, according to Bossuet, is the result of obedience, by power born of humility, by chastity which gives that fruitfulness to the faithful, living in the world, which is denied to sceptical and luxurious races. Saints, undoubtedly, need power from on high, to influence,

[1] That is, of those who are known, and who have allowed themselves to be known, thoroughly. See Mgr. Dupanloup's striking letter at the beginning of Mgr. Bougaud's "Life of St. Chantal," on the proper way of writing the lives of the saints.

as they do, men and the things of this world. But it is not by any means clear, that this power is not bestowed upon natural gifts which must needs exist before they can be metamorphosised by sanctity. Why should mental gifts be the monopoly of those who deal with external facts and abstract truths? Why should not a clear knowledge of one's own defects, a delicate perception of moral danger, a power of developing the natural faculties of the soul after the pattern of their divine ideal—why, in short, should not goodness be a matter of intelligence?

Socrates, if he could return to earth at the present moment, would be the last to deny the value of self-knowledge, for he summed up the whole of philosophy in those two words. To put it more simply, faith, hope and charity are the great springs of action in the lives of the saints. Catholic theology teaches that these three virtues come from God, but it also teaches that they need the co-operation of the natural virtues. The doctors of the Church have borrowed the names of these natural virtues from pagan philosophy. They call them cardinal or fundamental virtues: prudence, fortitude or strength of soul, temperance and justice.[1]

We may expect, therefore, to meet with these

[1] According to Benedict XIV. (II. 21), these four virtues must be visible, in an eminent degree, in the life of the servant of God who is to be beatified. I am not dealing with the theological question of the connection between natural and supernatural virtues, and the transformation effected by grace, etc. I am merely stating the fact that the possession of the one does not dispense from the necessity of possessing the other, in the case of saints any more, and I ought to say still less, than in our own.

latter virtues in the lives of the saints, even while, as yet, they have given small sign of their future sanctity. Not that these virtues are at that time fully or even equally developed, for sanctity often requires conversion and the abandonment of the state of life up till then adhered to. The saints have not all begun life like St Aloysius Gonzaga. Take, for instance, St Mary Magdalen, St Mary of Egypt, St Afra, St Margaret of Cortona, who were courtesans, St Paul, who was a persecutor, St Augustine, who had many sins on his conscience, St Francis Borgia, whose ingenious method of curing himself of an immoderate love of wine Liebnitz is so fond of quoting. There are saints too, who did not wander quite so far, but who, nevertheless, had to struggle against fiery passions. Bernard, the future Abbot of Citeaux, in order to get rid of a temptation caused by a single look, threw himself into a pond and stayed there until the icy water had cooled the ardour of his senses. St Vincent of Paul, incredible as it may seem, was " naturally of a bilious temperament and very subject to anger." We should be inclined to doubt his testimony of himself, if his friend and disciple, Abelly, did not tell us the same thing.[1] St Francis of Sales, as everyone knows, was naturally extremely passionate.

We see by these examples, and many more which

---

[1] St Vincent says more.—He tells us that had it not been for divine grace, he would have remained "in temper, hard and repellent, rough and crabbed." More than one of my readers will be inclined to think that, to use a familiar expression, the saint is " laying it on."

we have not time to quote, that easy temperance and absence of desires and passions are not necessarily among the natural virtues that sanctity builds upon. M. Renan has tried to make out that David was a ruffian, but he has been unable to deprive him of his largeness of heart and his tenderness, so wisely and sincere, even in the midst of crime. Christ, when He was on earth, forgave the debauchee, far more readily than He did the miser, and St Augustine was only interpreting His Doctrine when, later on, he dared to write, " Love God and then do what you like." The meaning of the saint's words is not difficult to understand. Love alone can suggest sacrifices and love alone gives the soul strength to carry them out.

But if sacrifice is the proof of love, must not the saints have had a good deal to sacrifice to God?

It is quite certain that the natural joys which the saints renounce, have not, in the first instance, been denied them by nature. The illnesses from which they suffer are the result of voluntary sacrifices, austerities, interior struggles, moral conflicts and the persecutions which have always fallen to the lot of saints, not of constitutional infirmity. These things they look upon as a "gift" from God, who, when He sees them determined to aim higher than the ordinary run of men, "visits" and "tries" them. We do not find one who chose sanctity as his line, because he was naturally delicate and unlikely to live long. The saints who died young, usually died a violent death. Among those who were not strictly speaking martyrs, cases of longevity are by no means

HUMAN NATURE IN THE SAINT

rare. St John the Evangelist lived to close upon a hundred, and so did the celebrated Fathers of the Desert, St Simeon, St Paul the Hermit, St Anthony, and later on St Bertinus. St Romuald and St Maurus lived to a still greater age. St Jerome died at seventy-two, St Augustine at seventy-nine, St Remigius at eighty-three, St John Climachus at eighty, St Vincent Ferrier at seventy, St Francis of Paula at ninety-one, St Vincent of Paul at eighty-five, St Philip Neri at eighty, St Paul of the Cross (canonised by Pius IX.) at eighty-two, St Peter of Alcantara, whose penances, St Theresa tells us, were "incomprehensible to the human mind," lived to sixty-three, and so did St Bernard and a crowd of others.

I should not be surprised to find that women saints, who lived a more sedentary life and made up, by penance, for the want of exterior heroism denied them on account of their sex, were shorter-lived in consequence. St Catherine of Genoa, however, whose physical sufferings were only equalled by the ardour of her love, reached the age of sixty-three. St Theresa, whose only desire was to suffer or die, lived to over sixty-seven and St Jane de Chantal to seventy; the greatest of all contemplatives, St Gertrude, was seventy when she died, for her biographers tell us that she was elected abbess at the age of thirty and held that office for forty years. Among the saintly personages of our own century, we may mention Mére de Lales Chappius, whose beatification is hoped for by the diocese of Troyes. She died at the age of eighty-two.

If, as we have seen, grace finds more to work

upon in the saints than an empty receptacle or inert and passive material, we must expect to find that each saint has his own individual character and temperament. The difference, in this respect, between St Peter and St Paul, is proverbial, and each, in consequence, probably had his own manner of governing and directing the Church. The former, "under the influence of grace, remained by instinct and nature, such as he is described to us in the Gospel, good, timid, generous and prompt in his impulses and thereby subject to lively impressions to which he yields instantly. One moment throwing himself out of the boat, full of faith which supports him on the waters, the next instant, doubting and missing his footing as easily depressed as he is consoled." Of the latter it has been truly said: "The nature of the scribe, although crushed, still survives under the action of the grace which has mastered him: there is the same soul, the same fire in his words, the same spirit in his actions."[1]

Throughout the history of the Church, there would seem to have been two distinct classes of saints. There are saints who personify active love and tenderness and there are saints who personify energetic action and the spirit of eager propagandism. We contrast St Francis of Assisi and St Dominic, St Bonaventure and St Thomas Aquinas, St Vincent of Paul and St Ignatius, in the same way as we contrast Bossuet and Fénelon or even Raphael and Michael Angelo, Mozart and Beethoven. In the case of saints, the difference

[1] Abbé Fouard. See work already quoted.

shews itself far less by opposition and controversy, than by the need they had of one another and the mutual help they gave each other. Had Bossuet and Fénelon been saints as well as great bishops and geniuses, instead of writing against one another, they would have felt impelled to meet in some lonely retreat, in order that, like St Dominic and St Francis, each one might gain from the other what he lacked himself.

These opposite characters, which yet perfect and complete one another, are to be met with, where least one should expect to find them—in those states to which the soul attains when it has struggled to rid itself of all attachment of the senses, all personal inclinations and even choice. One would easily think that all traces of natural character would be obliterated, when the soul has passed through the "night" of the senses and the night of the spirit, and has "bound" its faculties in order to subject itself more entirely to the action of God whom it contemplates and to whom it has given itself without reserve. And yet the great mystic retains his own individual character, which latter is discernible, we will not say in the doctrine which he teaches, but in that particular way of regarding all doctrine which he seems naturally drawn to insist upon. All students of the mystics have recognised this fact. St John of the Cross and St Theresa, St Francis of Sales and Saint Jane de Chantal were not only friends but fellow-labourers, both in action and in the doctrine which they meditated, applied, defended, wrote upon, and propagated. And strange as it may seem, the man and the woman who reformed Carmel, and the founder and the foundress of the Visitation, belonged, apparently, to rival schools of mysticism.[1] I say apparently, because nothing was omitted, still less misunderstood by the members of either group. The two alternating conditions of the mystical life, painful desire and joyous possession, were fully recognised by all of them. Still St John of the Cross and St Jane de Chantal dwell more particularly upon the necessity of enduring the desolation, aridities and sufferings which they had to go through themselves, while St Theresa and St Francis of Sales tell us more of the delights and the sweetness for which they, nevertheless, had to pay pretty dearly.

Historically, they form two groups, in each of which there is a joyous consoler and a wounded struggler. In the holy rivalries of the supernatural life, as in the greatest friendships known in the history of the world and of literature, contrast is as necessary to the mutual reformation of character as to the charm of mutual love.

It is difficult to tell exactly how far the natural character of the saints influences and determines their work. "When God wishes to make use of the saints for His glory He exercises them in various ways, so that He may mould them according to His own mind. He takes account of their natural dis-

---

[1] Père A. Poulain, S.J., "The Mysticism of St John of the Cross," 1893. A most interesting little work, as is also the book published about the same time by Père Ludovic de Besse: "Light thrown upon Mystical Works of St John of the Cross."

HUMAN NATURE IN THE SAINT

positions only just so far as to avoid doing violence to them."[1] Bossuet's own natural character inclined him to leave the least possible scope for the action of natural disposition in the saints. He loved absolute obedience far more than he did "theories." His contemporary, M. Olier, in spite of his austerity and his spirit of detachment from the things of this world, takes a wider view of the subject. In his opinion, in order to become a saint, it is not enough to have a sort of general inclination towards piety, love of God, and rectitude of life. "Otherwise," he says, "every Christian who is convinced of the beauty and holiness of the Gospel teaching would have a vocation to be a saint." "No," he continues, "over and above the call to aim at perfection which constitutes a religious vocation, these great souls have an interior drawing and inclination for the state of life they have chosen."[2] Elsewhere he expresses himself even more clearly. "God did not treat St Theresa in the same way as He treated St Gertrude, or St Catherine of Siena in the same way as St Theresa, or again St Catherine of Genoa in the same way as St Catherine of Siena, and yet He treated them all according to the interior dispositions which He found in each."[3]

M. Olier mentions St Catherine of Siena. She loves to dwell upon the diversities which exist in the mystical life, and she makes use of expressions which would have delighted Liebnitz as shewing meta-

---

[1] Bossuet, Sermon for the feast of All Saints.
[2] Letters, Lecoffre, I. 548.
[3] Letters, Lecoffre, II. 482.

physical intelligence in the necessary "discernment" of things. Some one of our contemporaries might, on the other hand, see in her words, only the æsthetic appreciation of the variety of expression inherent in beauty, common to nearly all Italians. "The saints," she says, "who enjoy eternal life have all followed the way of charity, only in a different manner, as they are not all alike. This same difference exists among the angels, who are not all equal. One of the joys which our souls will have in the next life will be to contemplate the greatness of God in the variety of the rewards which He will bestow on His friends. There is this same variety in created things which all differ from one another, and yet God has created them all from the same motive of love."[1]

Nature has so much to do with these innate diversities that we often find the characteristics of a certain family or city reproduced in the saint. The gentle virgin of Siena used to tell her fellow-townsmen that there were "no people so easily led by love as they," and she urged that this characteristic of theirs might be made use of in order to win them over to the cause of the reform of the Church and the pacification of Italy.[2] Later on, St Bernardine of Siena tells us the same thing. *Il sangue sanese e uno sangue dolce.* It is easy, therefore, to understand why, in spite of her austerities and her ecstasies, and all through her difficult negotiations for peace, the gentle saint never loses her love of flowers and her delight

[1] Letters—French translation in 8°, Poussielque edition, II. 124.
[2] *Id.*, I. 64.

in nature and in the scenery which glowed under Tuscan skies. She was fond of sending her friends bunches of flowers gathered with her own hands. She covered the little children with kisses, and, when called to assist a youth who had been condemned to death, she not only accompanied him to the block, but she spent the whole night previous to the execution in his cell, even allowing him to rest his head on her breast.

St Theresa was another great lover of Jesus Christ, but in her way of showing her love we recognise her Spanish blood. Her birthplace was Avila, surnamed Avila of the Knights. The women of that town stood a siege in the absence of their husbands, and their brave commandress had conferred upon herself and her descendants the right of voting in the public assemblies. The saint may have had these events in her mind when she described so naturally the fortress on the top of which she has planted the "banner of God," and when she spoke of women who were so full of the Apostolic spirit that they envied the liberty enjoyed by men of serving "the God of battles" in the midst of this world. There was nothing combative about her, however, nor did she love to rule and despise her own sex. "My son," she said one day to a religious, "when I was young I was told I was beautiful, and I believed it; later on I was told I was wise, and I believed that too, far too readily. I have often had to accuse myself in confession of these two vanities." Even when favoured with ecstasies and the most sublime revelations, she never forgot that she was a woman. She was even, in a sense, grateful to God for having created her one. She was of opinion that men received the favour of rapture and union less frequently than women, and she tells us, not without a spice of fun, that the reasons for this, divined by herself and those given her by St Peter of Alcantara, were all to the advantage of women.[1] She was naturally as proud as she was shrewd, loving and attractive; and so careful of her honour that, even at the time when she still loved the world and the reading of romances, that feeling was strong enough to protect her against temptations and even importunate imaginations. When, in later years, our Lord said to her, "My honour shall be your honour, and your honour my honour," it may well have seemed to her that she guarded both with the same confidence and noble sense of security with which, in former days, she watched over her own youth![2] Her dislike of the "way of fear," and especially of "servile fear," in the service of God, came, in great measure, from the natural character which she had inherited. She wishes us to follow in Christ's footsteps with "manly courage," an expression she constantly uses, and she was fond of saying that He ought to be served "gratuitously," as great nobles serve their king.

These differences of character are conspicuous in small things no less than in great. But are there small things in the saints? No doubt there are,

[1] Life written by herself, Lecoffre, p. 526.
[2] "I never felt in myself the smallest attraction for anything that could have sullied my innocence."—*Id.*, p. 19.

if by the word "small" we do not mean to imply censurable things and if we remember the childlike innocence that Christ held up as a model to His disciples. Many of the saints had simple tastes which they would have been ready enough to give up had the sacrifice been asked of them, but which they indulged, in matters of indifference or at times of recreation.

Many of them were lovers of the arts, which is not surprising as Catholic ritual necessitates the cultivation of nearly all of them. But apart from its connection with the ceremonies of the Church, many of the saints were passionately fond of music. St Francis of Assisi was so enthusiastic about it that he imitated little children and took a piece of wood and a ruler upon which he pretended to play the violin as a sort of accompaniment to the ideal music with which his entranced imagination was filled. Bartoli tells us that St Ignatius of Loyola was also ravished out of himself by music, to such an extent as to become unconscious of pain. Flowers delighted him so when he looked at them that it used to astonish the Fathers who lived with him.[1]

More than one saint has amused himself by playing and conversing with animals. St Francis' love of animals and especially of doves is well-known. He used to have nests made for them so that they might rear their young in the neigh-

---

[1] I have been allowed to touch the little flute and tambourine which St Theresa loved to play on feast days. They are still kept in the monastery of St Joseph at Avila.

bourhood of the monastery. St Philip Neri was devoted to his old cat and took the greatest possible care of it.

This latter saint is well known, too, for his eccentricities (Goethe, who was proud of having him for a patron saint, called them more respectfully " his whimsical sallies "). These sallies were, it is true, often full of good sense, as for instance, when the Pope sent him to visit a monastery in the neighbourhood of Rome in order to examine into the sanctity of a religious, said to be favoured with revelations and ecstasies. The weather was abominable and Philip, who had started on a mule, arrived at the convent, soaked to the skin and covered with mud. The sister was brought to him and she appeared full of sweetness and unction. By way of beginning his theological examination, Philip sat down, held out his leg and said to her, " Pull off my boots." The sister drew herself up, scandalised. Philip had seen enough. He seized his hat and went back to the Vatican, to tell the Holy Father that a religious, so devoid of humility, could not possibly possess the graces and virtues she was credited with.[1]

At other times it was his own disciples and children whom he liked to humiliate in public. If he saw that one of them was rather too pleased with his religious habit, donned for the first time,

[1] It seems that in our own times, a similar test has been held sufficient. A certain Rose Tamisier was supposed to be favoured with extraordinary graces. A prudent ecclesiastic came to see her. "You are the saint, aren't you?" he said to her. "Yes, Father," was the answer he got. The illusion was instantly detected.

Philip made him wear some ridiculous appendage —a fox's skin—tied to his back, and in this guise he would send him out for a walk in the streets. Another time he set his religious (oratorians and learned men) to rearrange all the kitchen utensils, and he often took part himself in these sanctifying though peculiar exercises.

His biographers are careful to tell us that these were inventions of his humility, which made him anxious to hide the treasures of holiness and learning which he possessed under a commonplace and almost foolish exterior. Goethe, in this matter, speaks like a regular hagiographer. " Neri summed up his principal doctrine in a short proverb: Despise the world, despise yourself, and despise being despised. And, as a matter of fact, this is the end of all knowledge. The pessimist often fancies that he has attained the two first points; to even aim at the third, one must needs have started on the road to sanctity."[1] I do not deny that there is a deep meaning and great truth in Goethe's words. His colossal genius enabled him to appreciate, and even to exaggerate, the contempt felt by the saints for all earthly things.[2]

---

[1] See *Journey in Italy*. Complete works, edit. Porchat, ix., 364 and foll.

[2] One might be inclined to think that Goethe wished to belittle his great patron, but nothing was further from his mind. This is what he says of him, and it is odd that his latest biographer should have passed it over in silence :—

" To strange and mysterious powers, he united the clearest common-sense, the justest appreciation, or rather contempt, of earthly things, the most active charity for the corporal and

Still, it is probable enough that Philip was acting, in a measure, according to the dictates of his natural temperament. Why not? On second thoughts, he may have seen, in this tendency of his, a means of checking the admiration men felt for him. We may even take that much for granted. But the first impulse must have been involuntary, for, whatever may be said of the love of humiliations indulged in by all the saints, we must allow that, as a rule, they do not invent such practices as these. They do not put themselves to the pains of acquiring artificial virtues. Take, for instance, a saint who is subject to abnormal absence of mind, like certain great students. He is glad enough to be laughed at for it, but he will not go and make believe to have distractions. Simplicity is ever a characteristic of the saints, even when raised to the most extraordinary states.

Much the same may be said of certain habits of cleanliness and (to give things their right names) of uncleanliness. The great majority of saints have

spiritual sufferings of his fellow-men. . . . He was most scrupulous in fulfilling all the duties of an ecclesiastic.   He devoted himself to the education of youth, taught them music and eloquence, suggesting themes both religious and ingenious, and encouraged conversation and debates proper for sharpening the mind. What is more singular still, he did all this of his own accord, and for years persevered in this line, without becoming a member of any order or being ordained priest. What is strangest of all, is that, in Luther's time and in the midst of Rome, one active, clever, pious, energetic man should have conceived the idea of uniting ecclesiastical and sacred with secular things, should have introduced divine things into secular life, and so should have prepared the way for a reformation."

certainly been advocates of the former. St Theresa returns again and again to the subject, and even inserted rules as to the obligation of cleanliness into the statutes of her order. She did not go quite the lengths of St Augustine, who would never eat with anything but a silver spoon, or of St Philip Neri, who could never bring himself to drink out of any but his own particular glass, and, what is more astonishing still, never used any but his own chalice in saying Mass. However, St Theresa would have agreed with St Bernard when he said, "Poverty I love, but not dirt," and she handed on her ideas to her daughters, as the following anecdote will show:—

St Theresa wished to make a trial, in the convent of Avila, of a new sort of habit, made of very coarse material. She used it herself at first, but not without suffering great inconvenience from it. At last she gave permission to the others to try it, as they were most anxious to do so. Worse results followed the general trial of the material, and a swarm of noxious insects made their appearance. St Theresa, who, like St Francis of Sales, ranked cleanliness among the smaller virtues, had not intended this kind of mortification to form part of the austerities of Carmel. She set to work to pray to the Lord to deliver them from the new plague of Egypt. While she prayed, the sisters went in procession, with the cross at their head, towards the spot where their holy mother was kneeling, singing the verse: "Since Thou hast given us this vesture, O King of Heaven, deliver our habits of serge from these insects."

Theresa caught up their words and improvised three more charming verses, which are given in the original account. Their prayers were evidently heard, and from that day to this all Carmelite convents, no matter how coarse the nuns' habits may be, are, by a special privilege, exempt from the attacks of these particular insects.[1]

What a contrast to St Benedict Labre, and how are we to defend his ways? We are not bound to believe that he was canonised because he treasured up what was so strongly objected to by the Carmelites of Avila. He had been disappointed in his early desire of becoming a monk of the Chartreuse, and he made up for the lack of a life of discipline and rule by treating his body with a contempt which may have been part of his natural character. If so, he turned it into a means of mortification, and, his motives being so high, he was thereby enabled to practise virtues which lent a value to that kind of resignation and asceticism which, in themselves, they certainly do not possess.[2] St John Chrysostom tells us that "the actions of the saints

---

[1] See Life of St Theresa by a Carmelite, I. 334.

[2] We must not, however, suppose that St Benedict Labre was altogether singular in this method of mortification, though he seems to have been eminent in it. The like is recorded of St Thomas of Canterbury and many another. We can only say that wisdom is justified in all her children, and that the same spirit may be embodied in very contrary manifestations. Still, though the spirit is from God, its expression need not be; nor are we bound to approve it any more than we are the style and diction of an inspired prophet whose literary taste may be very questionable.—*Editor's Note.*

were not all equally holy," and we may apply his words to the habits of St Benedict Labre as well as to the somewhat excessive refinement of St Augustine and St Philip Neri.

CHAPTER III

EXTRAORDINARY PHENOMENA IN THE LIVES OF THE SAINTS

SIMILAR discoveries will be easily made by anyone who takes the trouble to make a separate and careful study of the lives of the best known saints. The examples given above, are, however, sufficient for present purposes. Let us now see what effect their vocation, once solidly established, has upon the natural gifts of the saints. It does not, as we have seen, suppress them; but we should wish, if possible, to know how it contrives to work in harmony with them. The saint has renounced the joys of this world—or at least he has resolved only to use them with the greatest humility. He may have joined some community, whose members, though to all appearances vowed to the service of God, have no small share left of vanity and self-love, and in consequence he has had a harder battle than usual to fight, in order to purify himself and to influence his brethren for good. But he has at length destroyed everything that he has been able to detect in himself, contrary to the love of God and his neighbour, and henceforward he appears as if freed from the bondage of nature which he has, as it were, completely trampled upon. He continues, however, to live, think, imagine, act, to feel pleasure and pain, to suffer and to love. What has been the effect, upon these various faculties, of this transformation of his whole being?

We have already said that the saints are not necessarily persons of weak health, destined to an early grave. They are, however, subject to innumerable illnesses and they bless God for the trial. Some of these illnesses are of no psychological interest. Troubles of the stomach, and liver and lungs in their many varieties, are much the same in all men, and if sanctity counts for a good deal in the way we bear such pains, it does not alter the effects of the evil upon our nerves and muscles. There is one part, however, of our organisation which is more nearly affected by the soul and its operations, and that is our nervous system. Across its plexus the interchanging influences of our physical and moral being are for ever coming and going. It is the seat of those states of degeneration and nervous disease, which have attracted so much attention of late years.

As for nervous diseases, a certain critic has attempted, with the aid of recent psychological and medical theories, to prove that the most marvellous phenomena in the lives of the saints are due to them and to nothing else. Her task has been the easier as, by an error, excusable in the ignorant and less pardonable in the learned, these extraordinary phenomena have long been considered the dominating characteristic of sanctity. The saint was a man in whom the supernatural alone acted, and acted by means of an apparent upsetting of the ordinary course of nature. Therefore, men argued, if only science can be made to explain these so-called wonders by means of known pathological laws, the whole theological edifice sustained by the virtues of the saints will come down with a run. There was no longer any need to imitate Voltaire, to turn all evidence into ridicule and to bring accusations of hypocrisy against the most disinterested heroes of humanity. A natural explanation lay ready to hand —the facts, as facts, might be accepted: it was only necessary to explain[1] them and to wind up with a tribute to the artless simplicity of the "faith of the Middle Ages." It is a fixed idea in certain quarters that the "Middle Ages" alone had faith as well as a monopoly of simplicity, coarseness, and ignorance.

As an instance of what we have been saying, two doctors have been discussing the life of St Vincent Ferrier, in the *Revue Scientifique*.[2] He was a very celebrated "thaumaturgus" and one of those to whom tradition has ascribed the most miracles. Our two critics do not attempt to compare the degrees of authenticity of the different stories. They take them

---

[1] I use the word "explanation" of what hardly deserves the name. Some persons regard it as an axiom that in order to explain a fact one has only to bring it into relation with other already properly established facts. But to establish a fact and to explain it are two different things; and very often more general facts, by which it is sought to explain other facts, remain themselves unexplained. This is precisely the case with regard to the facts we are dealing with at present.

[2] Sept. 6, 1893. Article by Drs Corre and Laurent, entitled "La Suggestion dans l'histoire."

all together in a lump, and are evidently extremely delighted to come upon a sort of retrospective verification of their theories. They do not deny the facts, but they class them all as instances of lucidity or second sight, telepathy, hallucination, suggestion, or fascination. We are left to discover for ourselves (this essay being of a psychological character) what place these phenomena may have occupied in the mental and moral life of the saint.

Not only is it a fact that these phenomena are, by no means, one and all the distinguishing characteristics of sanctity, but many of them are to be found in both saint and sinner alike. Fortunately there are certain differences between the two cases, which it will be of interest to notice.

Penetration of the thoughts of others and what we call second sight is by no means a rare phenomenon in the saints. In St Catherine of Siena it was almost continual. It was very frequent in St Vincent Ferrier, and, according to the distinct evidence of her nuns, St Theresa had only to pass near one of them in order to guess her desires and temptations. By this means she was able to dispel them in some cases, and in others to gratify them by a definite refusal or promise of the desired permission. Is this kind of divination possible to ordinary mortals? If they are in the habit of living with another person and sharing their thoughts and feelings, certainly it is. A husband and wife are often struck with the same idea in matters concerning themselves and their children. A master can often guess what his inattentive pupil is thinking or dreaming about, if he has known him for a long while and if he is able to interpret the meaning, under given circumstances, of a pose, a gesture or a look. Certain nervous conditions may very possibly, with or without preparation, add exceptional keenness and delicacy to this kind of tact or clairvoyance.

We touch upon more mysterious ground than hitherto when we come to mental suggestions, a kind of experience which has been so persistently brought to light during the last fifteen years. It seems certain that hypnotised subjects divine many things. The brain, closed to the influences of the outer world, is acted upon solely by the hypnotiser. All their impressionability seems to be reserved for the invisible influences they receive from him. They not only obey his explicit and spoken commands but even silent suggestions made from a distance.

Is this the case with the saints? Hardly, for St Catherine of Siena, St Vincent Ferrier and St Theresa divine the thoughts, not of those who dominate them, but of those whom they dominate. They are, rightly, to be compared not to the hypnotised but to the hypnotisers. But the latter, even Charcot himself, whose experiences in this line have created so general an interest, are the 'divined' and not the diviners. Experimenters at the Salpetrière have even been accused of themselves producing, by involuntary action on their part, a great many of the disorders which appear in their patients.[1] It is not unlikely

[1] As I have said in a paper, dealing with this particular subject: "The person who is hypnotised, like the natural somnambulist, is endowed, for the time being, with an exquisite sensitiveness and

that the saints, upon whose souls worldly impressions have only a slight and passing effect, are gifted, in matters concerning conscience and the spiritual life, with a delicate sensitiveness to which the ordinary run of men are strangers. This transfer of sensitiveness, as it were, is only what one should expect to find. What is more, the saints do not use their powers of divination in insignificant and everyday matters. They come into play only when their sympathies as directors, reformers and apostles are aroused. Such a condition as this, manifested, as it is, by means of a superhuman charity, is no mere exchange of sensations between two nervous systems, one of which is disordered and overstrained by illness. It is the effect of a sympathetic charity which dominates the entire being and which is itself full of the Divine Spirit.

The above remarks will, we hope, help to explain certain facts in the life of M. Olier.[1] The first has reference to a lady, in all probability, Mademoiselle du Vigean. M. Olier, although at a great distance from her, was aware of a temptation which prompted her to abandon her religious vocation. He also knew of her delivery from this temptation and this is the account he gives of the way he came to know it. "In order to set me at rest about a trouble

delicacy of perception. Even from a distance, he is conscious of and is moved and acted upon by infinitely slight currents, in much the same way as a rheumatic patient in Europe is affected by the first beginnings of a change in the temperature, which have only really taken place, as yet, in America."—"Hypnotism and Suggestion": see the *Correspondant*, May 10, 1891.

[1] See *Lettres de M. Olier*, Paris: Lecoffre, I. 367.

which was causing me great pain, the Blessed Virgin explained to me the state of a soul, then in Paris, and who was, I feared, in doubt about her vocation. I saw her in a great state of delight and most extraordinary joy and jubilation; so much so that I said to M. de Bretonvilliers: I am no longer anxious about Mademoiselle du V.; she is in a state of great peace and joy. Two days later, I received letters from her, describing her state of mind, which was in every way similar to that which I had felt and experienced interiorly, in myself." In other words, the holy priest had, while thinking of this person, experienced a state of trouble or joy which convinced him that this state corresponded to the state of soul of the person for whom he was praying. In the same way, certain magnetisers who are more worthy of belief, tell us that when the true somnambulist thinks she has discovered the trouble from which the person who consults her is suffering, she has always first experienced it in herself. A slight suspicion of it reaches her which sets her overexcited imagination working. She vividly pictures to herself a state which, whether it be a reality or an illusion, becomes the starting point for a movement in an inverse direction. The thought of the somnambulist recurs to the person she has in her mind, and she attributes to him the same suffering or joy which she has just experienced in herself. It may be so. I do not vouch for the truth of this theory, although I admit that it is not utterly impossible. But the partial resemblance between the two states, even when granted, does not exclude differences:

the class of subjects acted upon is different; the agents who produce the two states are different; the end sought is different and the results obtained are also very different. We see this from the account of the close union of thought which existed between M. Olier and Marie de Valence. "I was conscious in myself," says M. Olier, "of the presence of this soul, who made me experience her state and interior dispositions, making known to me the design of God, which was that I should become a sharer in her spirit and her life."[1] His biographer confirms these words, by explaining to us how the fruit of the union between these two souls was that one communicated to the other the same intense devotion to one of the mysteries of our faith.

It will hardly be matter of astonishment after this to find that some persons see and hear things which are taking place at a great distance.

Many perfectly well authenticated instances of this are to be found in the lives of the saints. B. Raymund of Capua tells us that, while in Genoa, he distinctly heard the words of the message which St Catherine of Siena sent him from her death-bed in Siena.[2] "I heard a voice which was not in the air, speaking words which reached my mind and not my ears, but of which I was more distinctly aware, interiorly, than if they had been spoken by an exterior voice. I do not know how to describe this voice, if that may be called a voice which has no sound. This voice spoke words and conveyed them to my mind. ." On the other hand, those who assisted

---

[1] Letters, I. 429.   [2] In his *Legend*, iv. 4.

at the saint's death-bed repeated her words and Raymund recognised them as the very same words that had reached his soul.[1]

The vision of St Theresa is still more wonderful.[2] On July 26, 1570, while in prayer, she was transported to the high seas, where she was present, in spirit, at the death of forty priests and novices of the Society of Jesus, who were massacred by corsairs on the ship which was taking them to Brazil. She heard the voices of the victims and, amongst them, she recognised that of her kinsman, Francis Serez Godoï. When the vision disappeared, she told Father Balthazar Alvarez what she had seen. A month later, when the news of the martyrdom became officially known in Spain, Father Alvarez recognised the accuracy, down to the smallest details, of the account given him at the time by the saint.

It is impossible to deny that very similar facts are related in the history of hypnotism, suggestion and all kindred phenomena.—One has only to read the very careful accounts published by the *Psychical Research Society*, which reckons among its members, past and present, Prof. Balfour Stewart, Mr Gladstone, Mr Ruskin, Lord Tennyson and Mr Alfred Wallace, and amongst its correspondents in France, M. Taine and MM. Th. Ribot and Charles Richet. This Society has accepted as conclusively proved

---

[1] "Tell him that he is never to lose courage. I will be with him in the midst of all perils—if he falls I will help him to rise again."

[2] See *Bollandists*, Nos. 502, 509, 510.

seven cases of the appearance of individuals alive at the time, but absent, in reality, from the place where they were seen. In these seven cases there is an entire absence of any trace of charlatanism, madness or even chronic nervous disorder. Even so incredulous a mind as Scherer is forced to admit that these researches were conducted with caution, care and discernment, and he adds that the facts he is engaged in analysing are of such a nature as to greatly enlarge the scope of our psychological ideas.

Are we then to suppose that the phenomena related in the lives of the saints serve only to confirm the truth of the discoveries made by the psychologists of our own day, or that *vice versa*, the purpose of the latter is to obtain credence for the tales of hagiographers? Both are plausible assertions, but they are both calculated to offend those who prefer to attribute to supernatural agencies every single action of God's most favoured servants. But this latter opinion is neither that of the Church nor of the saints themselves. It is an undoubted fact that nature is constantly mingling itself with the supernatural through the whole of their lives. St Theresa expressly says so over and over again. We have every reason for believing that cases of second sight and of interior sight occur both with the saints and with persons in no way better than ourselves. As regards the latter, to what extraordinary combination in the effects of natural laws these phenomena—which they may have experienced perhaps once in their lives— are due, no one as yet knows. There is no evidence to shew that they were invalids or even nervous subjects like those whose cases are studied in hospitals. The present comparison is therefore of no avail for establishing the likeness between sanctity and nervous disease. And yet, on the other hand, the phenomena recorded by purely psychological societies have apparently no useful end in view. They are due to no patriotic, humanitarian, fruitful inspiration, to use the word in its strictly natural sense. They are merely singular occurrences, as yet unexplained, like many another before them, which must have passed unobserved by our ancestors. But in the saint clairvoyance is not to be disassociated from the sanctity which precedes and follows it and which gives it all its significance. There is a connection between this marvellous gift and the whole life of its possessor, his intimate friendships, his mission in the Church and the cares of his apostolate, which justifies us in regarding it as a result and a manifestation of his sanctity.

The same may be said of revelations, which are often accompanied by visions and apparitions of Christ and the Blessed Virgin, or of some saint, living or dead, to another saint. Legends are full of them, it is true, but a considerable number come to us on very trustworthy authority, as, for instance, those which St Theresa relates of herself. From a purely human point of view, I know of no evidence worthy of credence on any subject, if we are to reject that of the great Carmelite saint, which she gives with so many precise distinctions and luminous explanations. While analysing these phenomena, she repeatedly tells us that they do not all come from God, but that they are frequently caused by the Devil and the weakness of our own nature. Her great friend, St John of the Cross, insists even more strongly on this point, that visions, revelations and all exterior phenomena, like suspensions and the stigmata, are graces which are subject to a thousand dangers, imitations, and illusions. In the words of a learned Jesuit commentator upon his doctrine:[1] "If there is an author who is absolutely incapable of stirring up the imagination in favour of visions and revelations, that author is St John of the Cross. He has a positive aversion for such things, not only because the Devil and our own imagination are able, by their means, to trick us in a thousand different ways, but also because his absorbing idea is to get rid of everything which is not God Himself."

More than anyone else, St John of the Cross has laboured to impress upon men the real teaching of Catholic tradition, that phenomena of this kind do not constitute sanctity. We may go further and say that in those centres which produce saints, and where saints are most honoured, these occurrences always, in the first instance, create distrust and suspicion. What is feared is that they are either caused by disease, or that they will end by producing it on account of the too great strain to which they subject the mental and physical organisation of the person who experiences them. According to the teaching of St John of the Cross, the least unfavour-

[1] R. P. Aug. Poulain. *La Mystique de St Jean de la Croix*, p. 44.

able judgment that can be passed on them is that no one ought to shew animus against or ill-treat persons subject to these states. All that is necessary is to warn them of the dangers they run and gently to turn their attention to other things. We read in the *Ascent of Mount Carmel*[1] that "these souls should be led by the way of faith and be taught, by degrees, to disregard these supernatural impressions. They should learn to strip themselves of them for the sake of their own greater profit in the spiritual life. It should be explained to them that this way is the better one and that one single action, one single movement of the will proceeding from charity, is of more value, and is more precious in God's sight than all the good put together which they may hope to derive from their revelations. What is more, many who have never received these gifts have become incomparably more holy than those who have received them, in abundance, from Heaven."

St Jane de Chantal,[2] in one of the most interesting of her letters, expresses a similar opinion. She is speaking of a nun who had revelations and ecstasies. Madame de Chantal, at first sight, thinks there is something suspicious about them for the very reason that they are so frequent. She goes on to give an account of another girl, whose apparent sanctity deceived her confessor, the nuns and even the girl herself, for "she was the first to be taken in . . there being no other fault in her, but a certain pleasure she felt in imagining herself to be a saint and the vain amusement she took in her own

[1] II. 22. [2] Letters. Barthélemy edition, II. 499.

vain imaginings." These increased to such an extent that sensible people began to suspect her, and at last it was found out that there was nothing in her but "a heap of false visions." Consequently, the friend of St Francis of Sales comes to the conclusion that in the case before her they ought to shew "an absolute indifference and contempt for her imaginary visions and to talk to her of the solid virtues and perfections of religious life and in particular of the simplicity of faith in which the saints lived, without visions or revelations of any kind, being satisfied with believing firmly in the revelation contained in Scripture and in the doctrine of the Catholic Apostolic Church." Benedict XIV. says precisely the same thing when, after speaking of the visions of St Catherine of Siena and of St Bridget, he goes on to say: "Even though many of these revelations have been approved, we cannot and we ought not to give them the assent of Divine faith, but only the assent of human faith, according to the dictates of prudence, whenever these dictates enable us to decide that they are probable and worthy of pious credence."

What, we may ask, are we to go by in deciding whether or no a revelation is worthy of pious credence? First, the nature of the revelation or vision itself, but far more the character of the individual who is favoured with it. As we have seen by the verdict given by St Jane de Chantal, great frequency is a suspicious sign, and it is easy to see why. Habitual repetition suggests that, a new nature has taken the place of the former slowly acquired condition of the person. This new nature is an entirely different state in which the person is endowed with attributes of another order which manifest themselves by a sort of interior necessity. A metamorphosis of the description is open to two hypotheses. Either there has been a disturbance, entirely pathological in kind, like mental alienation, which creates a radical change in the nature of the sick person, or else there has been a glorious transformation. Now, even in the case of the greatest saints and of the most sublime spiritual states, nature, though greatly strengthened, is still there, and sin is still possible. Saints tell us so themselves and they add that God bestows these favours as He pleases, either as a reward or as a trial or for the good of the Church, that He withdraws them when He chooses, for reasons known only to Himself, and that they are gifts " the real value of which will only be made known to us in the next world."[1]

But because habitual or frequent repetition suffices to render these phenomena suspicious, we are not to assume that rarity is an infallible sign of their being genuine. Sometimes a revelation is made to an ignorant, simple person or to a child which hardly knows its catechism. The contrast between the unexpected wonder and the simplicity and want of culture of the recipient, attracts the Church's notice. She waits, however, to see what course events will take—and it is upon the character of the results that she bases her judgment. At other times the character alone of the person will ensure, first of all respect, and then a reasoned acceptance of the

[1] See St Theresa, III. 97 and 549.

truth of the revelation. In cases of this latter kind we may say that it is the proved sanctity of the person which reassures men's minds as to the truth of the phenomena rather than the phenomena themselves which gain credence, be they revelations, prophecies, visions or any other visible favour. The same is true of miracles.

This latter assertion may be a surprise to some, but it is nevertheless in strict accordance with the tradition handed down by the saints and the sovereign pontiffs. Everyone is familiar with the Epistle of St Paul in which he says that it is of more importance to possess charity than to be able to move mountains. The following beautiful passage in one of St Gregory's letters to the monk, Augustine, is less well-known. "Remember that the gift of miracles is not given to thee for thyself, but for those whose salvation is confided to thee. There are miracles worked by the lost and we do not even know if we ourselves are among the elect. God has given us but one only sign by which we may recognise His elect, and that is that we love one another." Elsewhere the holy Pontiff distinguishes between two classes of miracles—corporal miracles, which are miracles properly so called, and spiritual miracles, which are virtues carried to the pitch of perfection and heroism. He says, "Corporal miracles, though they are a witness to sanctity, do not create it; spiritual miracles, which take place in the interior of the soul, are not exterior witnesses to a virtuous life, but they create it. The wicked may attain to the former; the latter can be enjoyed by the good alone. Therefore, dear brethren, do not attach value to that which we share with the lost, but love those other miracles of charity and piety of which I have told you. They are the more safe as they are more hidden, and they are the more rewarded by God because they serve less to win us glory from men."

Centuries later, Benedict XIV. makes the same remark, that miracles may be a sign of sanctity, but that they are not its chief and essential sign. He draws attention to the fact that the Old Testament saints worked most of their miracles during their life-time while the saints of the New Testament work most of theirs after death, that is to say, when they have been finally confirmed in grace. He goes on to say that "When enquiry is instituted for the purpose of beatification or canonisation, no examination is made of miracles until after the heroic virtues or the martyrdom of the servant of God have been proved. These virtues are the first and most decisive witness to sanctity; visions, prophecies and miracles are of only secondary importance, and they are absolutely ignored if proof of heroic virtues is not forthcoming."

When in this way we examine into the personal life of the saint, we see that these extraordinary occurrences and the miracles are not purely accidental manifestations of his virtue, and that it is not even a sufficient explanation if we consider the latter to be the foundation upon which all else reposes. We have already seen that in the saint there is a constant interchange of influences going on between his outer and inner activity, which influences place their seal upon these mysterious powers, the existence of which it is impossible to deny. The same is true of miracles, whether they be of an unmistakable kind or of that other sort which men try to explain away by identifying them with certain rare but natural exhibitions of the power of ascendancy due to an irresistibly inspired prestige and confidence.[1]

Besides the fact that his revelations are few and far between, the saint, as a rule, works but few miracles. The best authorities are agreed on this point, but we will only instance the Bollandists. In their life of their founder, St Ignatius of Loyola, they declare that he worked so few miracles, that it became a question whether he had ever worked any at all, and after quoting the passages from St Gregory the Great, given above, they add, "What miracles did St Augustine work, or St John Chrysostom, St Athanasius, St Gregory Nazianzen and St Gregory of Nyssa? Very few. St Augustine used to say that it was a far better thing to convert a sinner than to raise a dead man to life."[2]

"But," it may be asked, "do you believe that saints were able at will to work or not to work miracles?" "No, I do not." "Well then, if, as you think, God really acts in them, why should this higher intervention be limited either as to the

---

[1] The two kinds are easy to distinguish. In the second category we may place the cure of a great number of diseases, but not the sudden cure of the blind, and still less the raising of the dead.

[2] 784, E—— 787, c.

number or the greatness of the wonders which it works?" My answer is, that it is no business of ours either to increase or diminish the effects of this intervention, and I may also remind my questioner that our Lord Himself complained of those who asked wonders of Him before believing, and that His having done so is a lesson for us. It is a lesson which the saints who asked God to work this or that miracle by their means had learnt and certainly applied to themselves. Let us listen to what they themselves have to say and let us learn from them what were their maxims and traditions on the subject.

First and foremost, the saint holds that the gift of miracles is absolutely worthless, that it is either an illusion or else the greatest possible danger to its possessor, if it is not completely under the control of two virtues which are of far greater value: charity and humility. No one will be surprised, I think, that I place these two virtues side by side, for there is nothing so inimical to the love of our neighbour as self-complacency and, still more, pride. For this reason the saint fears that the frequency of so great a gift may increase the frequency of the temptations likely to accompany it. And yet his humility is, in a way, safeguarded, for, as we shall have reason to remember more than once, later on, the very sublimity of his intercourse with God and the very intensity of the love to which he strives to correspond, enable him to measure the depths of the misery of our fallen nature. If he has been raised so far above it, his ideals have also been proportionately raised, and therefore it is that the consciousness of the gift of which he believes himself wholly unworthy is so frequent a source of anxiety to him, especially during the active portion of his life: no slight proof, by the way, of the genuineness of the miracle itself.

The following story is told by the latest biographer of St Bernard. "One dark thought tormented him, and that was the recollection of the miracles he had worked. At last he spoke out to his travelling companions: 'How can it be,' he said, 'that God should use such a man as I am, to work these wonders. Generally speaking, real miracles are worked by great saints; false miracles by hypocrites. It seems to me that I am neither the one nor the other.'[1] Nobody dared give him the answer that was in the minds of all, for fear of offending his modesty. All at once the answer to the riddle seemed to strike him. 'I see,' he said, 'miracles are not a proof of sanctity, they are a means of gaining souls. God worked them, not to glorify me, but for the edification of my neighbour. Therefore, miracles and I have nothing in common with one another.'"

So much for humility. As for charity, the saints would fear to wound it, especially if they obtained or even desired one of these useless wonders which do not directly serve for the edification of one's neighbour.

Thus enlightened by personal experience, no one is more on the watch than the saint, to detect false sanctity and to avoid contagion from it. When St

[1] Abbé Vacandard. *Vie de St Bernard*, vol. II. 232.

Theresa first began to receive Divine favours and to be led by "extraordinary ways," she was tormented by the thought that she was like a certain poor Clare who, for thirty years, excited the admiration of all Spain,[1] but who, in the end, confessed that she had criminally deceived almost the whole of Christendom. She not only governed the poor Clares of Cordova, but she became the oracle of the convents in Spain. Princes, kings, and even bishops, consulted her on the affairs of their kingdoms and dioceses. She apparently revealed the most hidden secrets and made known events that were taking place at a distance. For instance, she saw Francis I. taken prisoner at Pavia, and Rome sacked by the Imperialists. Her predictions were accompanied by wonders that had nothing in common with the miracles of our Lord in the Gospel, for they filled men with astonishment, without enlightening souls or strengthening hearts. The deluded populace admired it all and Magdalen became more and more inflated with pride at the increasing veneration felt for her. On great feast days she went into ecstasies and was often lifted two or three feet from the ground. At last, one day in the year 1546, a ray of Divine grace touched the heart of this woman. To the consternation of everyone, she went and threw herself at the feet of the Visitor of her Order and confessed that she had shamefully betrayed the confidence of her sisters and the public by means of sacrilegious tricks and the help of the Devil. . . . She confirmed her first avowal. . . . She was sent out of

[1] Magdalen of the Cross, a poor Clare of Cordova.

the city to end her days as a penitent, far away from the cloister which she had disgraced. These events made a great impression on everybody. All Spain was horrified, says the writer from whose account we have been quoting.[1]

How different was the conduct of St Theresa. Far from seeking these supernatural gifts, she felt " more and more anxious," " her fears increased " (the words are her own) in proportion as she felt that what was taking place within her was above the capacity of nature. It was only after years of trial and struggle and by comparing reiterated experiences, that, reassured on the score of her own good faith, and vanquished by love, she gave way without fear and consequently without reserve. She was sure of God's love and sure of herself, and from that time onward there was no gift that she did not accept and describe and explain for the glory of the Church and the good of souls. She used them gratefully and we may even say, simply and familiarly, in the same way as she did those natural gifts of heart and mind which she had received in such abundance.

Few indeed of the saints have attained to the same state of clear and peaceful possession which this saint enjoyed during the last five years of her life. St Jane de Chantal had to endure spiritual trials in her old age, and had great difficulty in overcoming them. This difference—it would hardly be right to say, this inferiority—does not in the very least take away from her reputation as the foundress of many convents and the directress of so many

[1] *Life of St Theresa*, by a Carmelite, I. 145.

nuns, who was so well able[1] to shield other superiors from the dangers which accompany extraordinary gifts, and what she calls "the traffic in revelations." How forcibly she reminds one of them, that at the last day, many a prophet and worker of miracles will be declared a worker of iniquity. She is not speaking of false miracles and false prophecies, but of miracle-workers and prophets "who have not been meek and humble of heart," after the example of our Divine Master.

With regard to visions, revelations and miracles, it is certainly true to say that they are mainly due to an agency from above. Sanctity is discernible chiefly in the manner in which the person accepts these gifts and in the use he makes of them. It is apparently not quite the same in the case of those phenomena which are the consummation of so many efforts and desires in the life of sanctity, and which lead, through different degrees of prayer, to union, rapture and ecstasy. It will be well, therefore, if we now endeavour to penetrate into those hidden depths which are lighted up for us by the inner experiences of the saints themselves. There we shall probably discover the source of the part which nature plays in the wonders we have been considering above; for, as Benedict XIV.[2] tells us, visions and revelations are, as a rule, only given to those who have already experienced ecstasies and raptures.

Is every saint an ecstatic and is every ecstatic a saint? It is very certain that every ecstatic is not

[1] See Letters quoted, I. 500.   [2] *De Canon. SS.*, III. 49.

a saint. Alfred Maury, a well-read man, and a psychologist, who has often treated of these subjects, delivers himself as follows: "Theologians consider ecstasy to be one of the most signal favours which the Creator can bestow on a creature, and Rome has placed most of those who have experienced it on the list of saints." Nothing could be more untrue than the above remark. It is a commonplace saying in theology, that, in the canonisation of saints, no heed is taken of ecstasies, or, at least, they are never approved of as specially miraculous, unless they are accompanied by some unquestionably supernatural sign. But with the help of Benedict XIV. and the saints, whose experiences he sums up, let us enquire a little further into things.

In his treatise on beatification and canonisation he distinguishes three kinds of ecstasy: natural ecstasy, which is a malady; diabolic ecstasy, and divine ecstasy.

In order to discern one from the other, it is necessary to watch the symptoms which precede the phenomenon, those which accompany it, and the results of whatever kind which follow upon it.

If the ecstasy recurs periodically and at stated intervals, if, in course of time, the ecstatic becomes paralysed, or is struck with apoplexy or any similar disease; if the ecstasy is followed by lassitude, inertness of the limbs, heaviness of mind, intellectual density and loss of memory; if the countenance becomes pale and livid, and spiritual depression ensues, then we may be sure that the ecstasy was a purely natural one. We may be still more certain of it, if, in consequence of earthly desires being aroused, the person becomes subject to fits of grief and fear.

Diabolic ecstasy may be recognised if the subject is a man of bad life, or, if the attack is accompanied by excessive distortion of the limbs, by a disorderly (and not, as in the case of Divine ecstasy, a merely unusual) bodily disturbance, and still more if these movements are in the slightest degree unseemly. We may suspect diabolic ecstasy if the person can bring on or arrest the attack at will, if he speaks like a man whose mind is affected, if it appear as though someone else were speaking with his mouth (*quasi alius loquatur per eum*), if, after apparent alienation of mind, he is unable to repeat what he has said, and lastly, if the seizure comes on frequently in public places, and in the presence of a crowd of spectators.

The absence of all of the above symptoms is a testimony in itself to the Divine character of the ecstasy. All doubts will vanish if the words of the ecstatic tend only to excite others to the love of God, and if, when consciousness returns, he shews himself to be more and more strengthened in charity, humility, and peace of mind.

Once admit that an ecstasy is Divine and it is easy to see how much it owes to a supernatural agency. If, as our religion teaches us, the least virtue requires the help of grace, how great must be the grace required to produce states such as these. There are, however, spiritual causes which effect a sort of personal preparation for this sublime state. Benedict XIV. tells us of three: intensity of admiration, greatness of love, and strength of exaltation or joy. This does not sound very much like the state of collapse which many people consider to be the chief characteristic of ecstasy. However, I foresee an objection. I shall be told that I ought to distinguish between the preparation for the attack and the attack itself; that, in all probability, while the attack is preparing, the vivacity of the feelings produces a great increase of brain activity beyond the ordinary powers of nature, but that this is precisely the reason why this state of exaltation should be followed, as a necessary consequence, by a state of complete exhaustion, and that the immobility of the body is a clear indication that the functions of life are, for the time being, at a standstill.

The experiences of the saints provide us with an answer to this objection. In all accounts given by them we are able to distinguish between two orders of faculties or operations. That the inferior operations, even breathing, are suspended, is true.—It is also true that this state of body may, according to the natural constitution and temperament of the person, be accompanied by phenomena which are absolutely similar to those produced by the different kinds of ecstasy doctors study and diagnose in their patients. But in the words of St Theresa, while the soul is asleep, as regards earthly things, it is awake to the things of heaven. "I have noticed," she says, "that the soul has never more light to understand the things of God, than in this sort of rapture."

"It is true," she adds, "that if anyone asks me how it is that, while our faculties and senses are as much suspended (in their operations) as if they were dead, we are able to hear or understand anything, I can only answer that this is a secret which God has reserved, with many another, to Himself." She is none the less positive that during a rapture, the soul feels itself to be illuminated: "The understanding stays its discursive operations, but the will remains fixed in God by love; it rules as a sovereign." It is then that the apparent vacuum in the mind is filled up by visions. They are sometimes purely intellectual visions, which are rather an intense realisation of the presence of God and of the ineffable effects which it produces on the soul. More often they are visions of the imagination and inward sense. The latter, though no doubt more liable to illusions, are more in keeping with the weakness of our nature, for when the vision ceases, the soul, with the help of the images which still remain in the mind, is more able to recall the vanished scene.[1]

We must not lose sight of these two characteristics of ecstasy in the saints: the sleep of the senses and the awakening of the higher faculties. If the former alone is present, it is a sign of false ecstasy; if the latter accompanies it and because it does so, we recognise Divine ecstasy.

[1] According to St Theresa, intellectual visions last longer, and when they are thus protracted, the state which accompanies them, cannot properly be called ecstasy. See III. 504, 511. *Cf.* Benedict XIV. III. 49.

However, someone may say that facts which are caused by the Devil or by a special intervention of Divine power are outside the sphere of science and have nothing whatever to do with psychology. This is a mistake. We shall be careful to keep well within the limits of the controversy, but still it is quite possible to avoid all discussion as to the nature and origin of the mysterious occurrences and yet to study how the human soul conducts itself, during and after the occurrence itself. A miracle does not arrest all the laws of nature in the subject in whom it is worked. The rod of Moses caused water to flow from the rock, but the water, thus miraculously produced, was subject to all the laws of weight and hydraulic action. The Labarum of Constantine, once it had appeared in the skies, shone according to physical laws and was seen according to the law of optics,[1] etc.

And so too, with regard to the extraordinary phenomena in false and true mysticism alike, the best authorities are agreed that in both cases there exists a fixed process, a connected whole, with which the unexpected occurrence blends itself without destroying the economy of nature nearly as much as is supposed. It is highly probable that this occurrence is the culminating point in a series of states[2] as well as the starting point in a series of others, and the same may be said of certain decisive actions in everyday life, which are dependent upon a more than ordinary exercise of our free-will. In

---

[1] See Appendix.
[2] This does not mean that they produce it of themselves.

like manner, modern pathology teaches that although the germ of disease may come from outside, it is none the less received by a prepared organism which, according to the manner in which it is disposed, either preserves and develops, or else eliminates it. Now take the case of the false mystic. Unable to control his imagination, excessive in his austerities, and therefore subject to melancholy, covetous of exceptional favours, undisciplined in prayer, more anxious to love and especially to think himself beloved, than to exercise himself in humility and patience, he, in a way, deserves to become the victim of illusions, and when they occur he does his best to prolong their disastrous effect upon his faculties. The true mystic, on the contrary, is humble and prudent and careful to preserve a just balance in all things. He is convinced that he ought to offer as well as ask, to give as well as receive, and therefore he "devotes himself to the service of God with manly courage."[1] He will not acknowledge the Divine nature of his own visions, excepting in so far as they enable him to advance in virtue. He knows very well that, in the matter of his own perfection, however large a share in it he may ascribe to the action of God, he can never attain to it without personal effort. He perseveres in his efforts in spite of all the obstacles he encounters both in himself and in others.

He is well aware of these obstacles, for in this, no less than in other things, it is astonishing to see with what certainty, good sense and accuracy, the saints have detected, treated, and cured false ecstasy.

[1] St Theresa.

They know the symptoms well. That mixture[1] of physical weakness and dreaminess, that prostration of strength increased by a collapse of will-power, that melancholy in which the soul is either beguiled or tyrannised over by fixed ideas, those illusions of the imagination in which an ordinary fainting fit is mistaken for an ecstasy, that half wished-for state of delusion which is the offspring of a mysticism in which pride has too large a share, or of desires, ill-sustained by a defective energy and prudence. The saints have described all this, dreading it both for themselves and for those they had to direct.

It is really quite amusing to watch contemporary psychologists, those who confuse mysticism, of whatever kind, with sanctity, and endeavour to prove that all the marvellous gifts of the saints are so many illnesses to which mystics are subject. They discover a whole heap of things which the saints have all along known of and admitted. Human nature is ever the same. In the present day, as in every age, there are persons with diseased minds, who, instead of dreaming of earthly love and greatness, become enamoured of the melancholy joys of an imaginary intercourse with angels and the Deity. They are to be met with in all pious circles. Priests, whom they torment with their scruples and general unreasonableness, know them well. Why should

---

[1] In his Life of St Francis of Assisi (2 vols., Paris : Lecoffre), M. l'Abbé le Monnier gives the following as the saint's own words on the subject: " We must needs use great discretion in the way we treat our brother, the body, if we would not have it excite in us a storm of melancholy."—II. p. 395.

we hide the fact that there are some in convents, since St Theresa and St Jane de Chantal tell us that they found many in their own communities. They are constantly warning us against that evil system, which begins by unrestrained enjoyment of certain sensible spiritual joys, is continued by a half voluntary depression of spirits, is increased by want of nourishment, followed by growing physical weakness, until it ends in a kind of ecstasy which contains nothing but dangers.

The error we are endeavouring to correct consists in supposing that because this innocent but melancholy imitation of sanctity exists, therefore it is the habitual state of real saints. This kind of reasoning is on a par with the logic of those who imagine that because certain intemperate habits are common among third-rate authors and artists, therefore, as a necessary consequence, these habits are a component part of true genius.[1]

I have no wish to deny that these disorders of the nervous system, these violent attacks of pain, alternating with insensibility, followed by complete prostration of strength, are sometimes to be met with in the lives of the saints. Several have given us an account of their sufferings in this respect. They speak quite openly and enter into the minutest

[1] For instance, Lombroso, having met at Bergamo a man called Zola, who, according to him, was "a swindler and a man of genius," proceeded to draw from that fact a conclusion in favour of his theory that genius, crime and madness are all akin. The best of it is that he wrote a letter to the well-known novelist informing him of the discovery. (This letter was published in the *Archives d'anthropologie criminelle de Lyons*.) He honestly thought Zola would be flattered. See my *Psychologie des grands hommes*, 2nd edition.

details. For instance, St Theresa describes catalepsy with great accuracy—she is speaking from memory and from personal experience.[1] But, unlike false mystics, the saints do not attempt to hide the real nature of their sufferings. They neither turn them to account for purposes of self-glorification, nor do they make them serve as excuse for sitting down to a life of perpetual grieving and idleness. They often, it is true, recognise in them the handiwork of the Devil, who is allowed to try them as he tried the holy man Job. But frequently it is merely that weak nature has given way. They do not make a medical analysis of their case.[2] They are humble enough to admit that their nerves are not more invulnerable than their lungs or their stomach. They are perfectly aware that their symptoms denote illness pure and simple, and if the disorder continues for any length of time they set to work to seek a remedy for it.

And what kind of remedies do they go in for? St Theresa goes straight to the point—she never beats about the bush—and the most modern of doctors will find no fault with her remedies on the score of sentimentality. What advice does she give?[3] She has already spoken of those persons who, by reason of their austerities, prayers and night-watches, or

[1] See her Life, by herself, ch. xx.
[2] St Theresa, however, shews a complete grasp of the subject. As I have said elsewhere, she was far in advance of the science of her day, in the way she distinguished and analysed the four different kinds of melancholy recognised by science in the present day. Article on *Neurasthénie* in the *Quinzaine*, Feb. 1, 1897.
[3] III. 402, 403.

even only on account of the delicacy of their constitution, "are unable to receive any spiritual consolation, without being overcome. Directly they experience a certain joy in their souls, their bodies become weak and faint. They give way to a feeling of intoxication which increases as nature gets weaker and weaker. They persuade themselves that it is a rapture, but what they call rapture is mere waste of time and health. I knew a person who remained in this state for eight hours. Her confessor and many other persons had been deceived. But another person,[1] to whom God had given light, recognised the snare. Her advice was listened to, *the poor ecstatica was made to diminish her penances, to sleep more and eat more, and with the help of these remedies she was cured.*"

As for the saint herself, she does not wish to be cured.[2] Why should she? for first of all this temporary weakness of body caused by ecstasy is only partial with her and those like her, and secondly, it is in itself only a very short intermediate stage between two periods of intense spiritual activity. It is preceded by great energy of desire and followed by great energy of action. It is true that, during the holy ecstasy itself and immediately after it, the body is left without strength, but this is not because it has lost its powers of itself, but rather because the soul has " taken them away." And if the soul has taken them away, the result is

[1] The saint herself.

[2] I am of course referring to her mystical experiences taken as a whole, and to her spiritual intercourse with God, not to the attacks of fever and other sufferings to which she was subject and for which she allowed herself to be treated just like anyone else.

not by any means pure loss, as we have already seen. They are drawn off from the body and concentrated in a piercing intuition, in a complete and most generous offering of the whole being and in acts of most ineffable desire. From this, as from a source, they slowly filter back through the different faculties, which they fill with delights, until they reach even the body, giving back to it far more than had been taken away from it, for "though the body is often infirm and full of suffering before ecstasy, it comes out of the ecstasy full of health and admirably prepared for action."[1] This is the state produced by really Divine ecstasy. The soul *in the end* finds herself more free, more full of peace, and stronger, and the body shares in this complete recovery of health.

But was this a special favour reserved to St Theresa? Was it the result of her Spanish temperament and that original strength of constitution which enabled her, in spite of her illnesses (and of her doctors, some of whom were amazingly stupid), to reach the age of seventy? No, for we notice exactly the same thing in St Catherine of Siena, who was delicate and died young. We know that while in ecstasy she dictated or wrote many letters. We also know which they are, as her confessor, Raymond of Capua, and her secretaries kept count of them. They are full of intelligence, firmness, and courage, and also of the fervent piety of the true contemplative. They are remarkable, too, for the wisdom of the advice she gives in them, to the Pope,

[1] St Theresa, her life, 208.

the magistrates of Siena, and to princes. For in one she treats of the duties of married people, in another of justice, and they nearly all of them bear reference to the maze of political difficulties from which she succeeded, almost single-handed, in extricating her country and the Church.

It is not in other people alone that the saints have been able to detect and expose false ecstasy. We understand in our neighbours only what we have, in some degree at least, experienced in ourselves. I particularly wish to be rightly understood here. I do not mean to say that there was a mixture of truth and error in the saints, nor do I mean that they were subject alternately to real and counterfeit ecstasy. I only wish to say two things: first, that, as they admit themselves, they were conscious, no doubt to a lesser and lesser degree as they advanced in life, but still they were distinctly conscious of what they call the threats and power of the devil; and secondly, that their ill-health often brought them to the verge of those purely natural states into which they saw others fall, for a longer or a shorter time, or perhaps for life.

In other words, while the weak succumbed to the danger, the saints triumphed over it. But they triumphed at the cost of having realised the nearness of the evil and of having manfully fought against it.

It was a favourite saying of St Theresa and St Jane de Chantal that we must never judge of a phenomenon, or a state of soul, or a way of life, by its beginning, but only by its continuation and principally by its end. An impulse may come from nature, and yet rectify itself and end by leading us to God; and again the impulse may be divinely inspired and yet afterwards deviate. Man is responsible for the rectification through humility as for the deviation through pride, and this it is which gives its dramatic interest to the lives of the saints.

Many, I know, will still be inclined to ask, " But why is it that phenomena, so widely different in character, shew themselves in saints and sinners alike ? Why do evil doers have visions and work miracles and why are God's elect brought in contact with the devil?" The simple reason is that without heroism there can be no sanctity, and there can be no heroism unless the victory is difficult[1] and costly. Nothing can be more mistaken than the idea that there is a gulf between the natural and the supernatural, that no inspired person can make a mistake, that no one, favoured with revelations, can misinterpret them; and on the other hand, that no one who has begun by yielding to morbid or diseased impulses, can ever, with the help of good will, transform them into truly spiritual desires. The saint has, at first, to pass through many states which bear a superficial resemblance to illness or evil. He is well aware that this resemblance, though unreal or doubtful at first, may, if he gives way to melancholy, vanity, and desire for a too sensible enjoyment of the favours he has received, increase and become real. On the other hand, however slight the difference may appear in the

[1] See Appendix.

beginning, it may go on increasing until the soul finds herself at the very opposite pole of psychological existence.

Therefore, I repeat again for the last time: in the matter of revelations, prophecies, visions, miracles, raptures, ecstasies and all kindred phenomena witnessed in the lives of the saints, it is not the extraordinary occurrence itself which is to be taken as a proof of sanctity, but it is the effective sanctity, the virtue which is in the heart and which manifests itself by works, that determines the real nature of the miraculous occurrence. It is true that the saints learn by experience to recognise those revelations which come from God. "The revelations which are from God," says St Theresa, "are recognised by the great spiritual treasures with which they enrich the soul."[1] And again, "Every desire which is from God is accompanied with light, discretion and wisdom." But elsewhere, the same saint tells us: "When a soul is truly humble, even if a vision came from the devil, it would do her no harm. But if she is wanting in humility, a vision, which had God for its author, would do her no good. If instead of humbling herself for having received such a favour she is puffed up by it, she will be like the spider which turns all it eats into poison, whereas, by humility, she might imitate the bee, which converts all it takes into honey."

I am inclined to suspect that some one of my readers, who is of a philosophical turn of mind will say "Oh, yes, certainly. Sanctity, of course, is in

[1] See her works, Vol. III., 4, 100, 108.

the will and heart of a person; humility is of far greater value than prophecies, and charity than miracles. But why not go further, why not admit that the saints drew all these great spiritual gifts, courage, light and wisdom, which they fancied they derived from an exterior inspiration and supernatural light, from their own inner consciousness, and that it is only an excess of humility which leads them to attribute these qualities to a mysterious intervention from above? What they believed to be the effect of visions and ecstasies was merely the exterior reflection of their own purity and love—in a word, of their own perfection, acquired after years of effort. We all of us, in this way, contain in ourselves, in our own dispositions, whether gay or sad, courageous or the reverse, the sources of that joy or sorrow which we imagine comes to us from outside, filling us, in spite of ourselves, with unexpected emotions."

I am not writing a controversial treatise, and therefore I shall not stop to demonstrate how Christian doctrine and Psychological truth both agree in teaching that interior things and exterior things, the action of man and the action of that which resists him or sustains and attracts him, are inseparable one from the other. All I say is: if you really believe that it is only humility which makes the saint attribute to grace from on high, that which is really the fruit of his own rich nature, let us have one of two things. Either let us hear no more about illness being the cause, whether direct or indirect, of the visions of the saints, or else be so good as to explain how so great a degree of spiritual well-being, with its attendant advantages, can possibly coincide with what is neither more nor less than a state of hallucination and disease.

We are now, I trust, in a position to understand how it comes about that serious and honest minds[1]

[1] I am referring, not only to doctors, but to a learned Jesuit, Père Hahn, whose work, "Hysterical phenomena and revelations," published in the *Revue des Questions Scientifiques* of Brussels (1883), was at first crowned by the Academy of Salamanca after a public disputation and considered by the highest ecclesiastical authorities in Spain as a great testimony in honour of St Theresa. Père Hahn's work was, nevertheless, placed on the Index. This does not mean that it was formally condemned, but only that it was considered to contain propositions insufficiently explained and calculated to mislead certain minds.

The Congregation of the Index does not give the reasons for its decisions, which are sometimes of a temporary nature and only intended to point out that the work contains some things which are dangerous, inopportune, or which need revision. But in the present case, this is what we may fairly conjecture :—

Père Hahn's chief theory is that as St Theresa was on the one hand subject to hysterical, and on the other to supernatural phenomena, she became so well able to distinguish between the two, that this twofold experience gives us, in her case, an unexpected and precious assurance of her accuracy. The experience she had had of the former order of facts helps to convince us that she is not mistaken when she describes the latter. She does not confuse the two as she is in a position to distinguish between them, and she distinguishes correctly. This theory was very acceptable to the Jury at Salamanca and received a majority of votes. It is not altogether unworthy of the reception it met with. Before coming across Père Hahn's work, I had myself advanced a similar theory in my first articles in the *Quinzaine*. I will now endeavour to put it in a more accurate, and if possible, more acceptable form.

have thought that they discovered signs of hysteria in the saints. It is also clear, I hope, that they made a very great mistake. We shall be forgiven, perhaps, for insisting strongly on this point, for herein lies the origin of the most subtle and difficult to meet of the many objections that have been urged against the true character of the saints.

Hysteria is a disease, but it is not a disease which is due to a merely accidental and passing weakness of body. It is a tendency, and unfortunately an

If we turn, however, to the *Revue des Questions Scientifiques* and read the article itself carefully, it is sufficiently obvious, to my mind at least, why the Index decided as it did.

The Congregation may, it is true, have thought that the ordinary reader would be misled by the word hysteria, which has so long been erroneously used to express a feigned intensity of temperament, and it may have considered that the learned Jesuit had, therefore, instituted a premature and inopportune comparison. But the article contained two other and more serious errors—

In the first place, the writer does not distinguish clearly enough between accidental phenomena which threaten illness, and the illness itself when completely established and developed in all its parts. A person can have pains and not be a confirmed gouty or rheumatic subject; or can be hard of breathing without being asthmatic; or can shew signs of the presence of sugar or albumen in the system without diabetes or Bright's disease following as a matter of course. The question lies entirely in this: Does he resist or succumb to the first symptoms when they appear?

Then again, Père Hahn greatly exaggerates the number and the nature of these accidental phenomena. The reader will agree that this is so, when I say that he tells us that St Theresa (who was so full of good sense and often of fun) had frequent attacks of melancholy, and in proof of this assertion, he quotes her account of the pain she felt on leaving her father's house to become a Carmelite. A man must really be over-anxious to prove his case when he sees symptoms of melancholia in so natural a grief as this.

extremely powerful one, to a chronic disorder which affects the whole system.[1] During the last few years, attempts, only partially successful, have been made to establish some kind of order among those innumerable nervous ailments which stop short of madness,[2] and the following is the conclusion arrived at with regard to the tendency which produces them.[3]

Healthy and normal vitality consists essentially in the progressive unification of the faculties, that is to say, in an ever-increasing co-operation and harmony between their various activities, conditions, and habits. The essence of morbid vitality—and according to present ideas, hysteria is its principal form—consists in the disassociation and disintegration of these same faculties. Worn out by some drain upon his strength, of which medicine has, as yet, discovered

---

[1] The disorder can no longer be called chronic, and it never really establishes itself, if it yields to medical treatment or to a successful reaction on the part of the healthy faculties. But if nothing occurs to stop it, it is bound by the law of its nature to develop fully. Moreover, it is extremely difficult to check a deviation which manifests itself by symptoms such as the following: perversion of sensitiveness, prolonged anæsthesia, loss of consciousness, modifications of the natural character, delirium of various kinds, epileptic attacks alternating with periods of lethargy.

[2] I have not thought it necessary to examine into the theory that saints and also great men are a species of lunatic. Some paradoxes may be safely left to die a natural death.

[3] Among the various works on the subject, I have selected two volumes of M. Pierre Janet's: *Etat Mental des hystériques*. Paris: Rueff, for quotation. They are very full, very clear, and most interesting. I intend to draw very largely upon them.

neither the working nor the seat,[1] the hysterical subject is no longer able, or, at best, only very imperfectly able—to reduce his recollections to order, or place them in their proper relations with his actual life. These recollections return haphazard to his mind, like an unruly crowd which declines to carry out any operation with attention and discipline, and in view of a given object. His will no longer acts in connection with reasoned ideas. Sometimes he acts in obedience to ideas suggested to him, which in medical language means, ideas which come to him suddenly from outside, without his knowledge or the co-operation of his will. These awake in him an irresistible impulse to pass from ideas to action. His will is usually dormant, and responds neither to reason nor to necessity. He can eat, digest, walk, until the fancy takes him that he cannot, and then he at once ceases to do any of these things, unless unconsciously, in a moment of distraction, or when under the power of a suggestion, which he can neither co-operate with nor resist. Every somnambulist is therefore, in reality, an hysterical subject at bottom, and every hysterical subject easily lends himself to the phenomena of artificial somnambulism. On the other hand, if he is told or he imagines that some one part of his body is more sensitive to pain than the other parts, he at once feels an extraordinary pain in that part, which communicates itself to the

[1] Professor Grasset of Montpellier makes out that this phenomenon is infectious; the nerve centres are poisoned and therefore disturbed and disorganised. A destructive action is set up owing to the presence of *toxine* microbes. This theory has gained considerable ground.

rest of his body. It is a case of self-suggestion certainly, though he is utterly unconscious of it, and he is as completely dominated by the idea as if it had been objectively suggested by an operator or a doctor.

In spite of these imaginary feelings, the field of consciousness of the hysterical subject, to use a technical expression, is narrowed. He continues to have ideas, but these appear to be located in a region which is new and superadded in him, and in which everything seems to act automatically. There ensues what is called a division of the personality. There is the former personality, and the morbidly produced personality. These two reveal themselves by turns, bringing in their train their respective separate recollections, and in turn mutually supplanting one another. Meantime, one fixed idea works itself out of this kind of struggle or anarchy, and what is often taken for imagination, cleverness or force of will, is merely passive obedience to this fixed idea. Under its influence, the subject affects feelings to which he is in reality a stranger. He acts as if these feelings were real. "He acts," says Charcot, "with an extraordinary cunning, sagacity and tenaciousness—but his only object is to deceive people, and he does so without need or motive, and often unknowingly." "In short," says M. Pierre Janet, "hysteria is a form of mental disaggregation, characterised by a tendency to a complete and permanent division of the personality."

After this, my readers will think that in trying to refute the idea that the saints were hysterical subjects, I am taking a leaf out of Don Quixote's book and tilting at a windmill. And yet, without going back upon Père Hahn's article, I will just take the following passage from the otherwise learned work from which I have been largely quoting. M. Pierre Janet gives us a passage from St Theresa in which she owns that one day, wishing to read the life of a saint, she read the same lines over four or five times without being able to catch the sense, and that she had to put the book down. "The same thing," she says, "happened to me several times." M. Janet tells us that this was a case of "aprosexy" (or incapacity to fix the attention), and he continues: "Hysterical subjects of our day follow in this as in other matters the example of their illustrious patroness. In fact, the best way of discovering simple cases of "aprosexy" is to get them to read a few lines attentively and then ask them to say what they have understood of them." He instances the case of a woman called Justine, whom he saw at the Salpêtrière, as another example of the same kind of thing.

If the mental condition of a person is to be judged of by accidents of this nature, brain doctors and neurologists will be able to enjoy a very large practice indeed. However, St Theresa and Justine were unlike in more ways than one, and consequently we shall be obliged to look a little more deeply and thoroughly into the question.

Are we really to believe that the saint who has sacrificed health, pleasure, riches, and worldly honours in order to follow his vocation, and who sees the latter confirmed by revelations and ecstasies, is subject to the same suggestions as those which are experienced by somnambulists and hypnotised persons? .We may at any rate safely assert that the manner in which the saint experiences them is different. As we have already said, these phenomena excite suspicion in the minds both of those to whom the subject confides his experience, and of those whose office it is to decide as to their true nature. But it is also certain that when the saints experience these phenomena, they are themselves very far from receiving them with the same unreasoning simplicity with which the sick person accepts the idea which has taken possession of his mind. The humility of the saint causes him to fear. He thinks himself unworthy of such a favour and he resists it as the token of a degree of love which he believes is utterly undeserved by him. The biographer of Blessed Margaret Mary gives the following touching account of her: After her profession, her soul continued to be filled with the same sweetness and consolation which she had experienced in the novitiate. This caused her surprise and she began to be uneasy. She had espoused a God who had been crucified, annihilated, despised and insulted, and she had no wish to be treated otherwise than He was. She complained to our Lord, "Oh my God," she said, "will you never send me sufferings."[1] Like St Theresa, she accused herself in confession of these graces, fearing that sin had crept in in their wake. She would not yield to her inclination, until she had received a reasoned-out

[1] Mgr. Bougaud. *Vie de Marguerite Marie*, p. 136.

and carefully explained permission to do so. Then, and not before, did she give herself entirely up to it.

St Theresa was so perfectly conscious in herself of the effects of these states that she not only describes them for us, but also analyses, explains and comments upon them. Her observations are often of a deeply metaphysical nature and she draws many very clear and precise psychological distinctions. She does not deny the existence of false visions, for she has experienced them herself, but she is on this account all the more alive to the contrast between the true and the false and the better able to distinguish between them: "Therefore,"[1] she says, "there is an immense difference between them and I do not doubt that even a soul which has arrived at only the prayer of quiet, is perfectly well able to distinguish one from the other. These visions have each their characteristic marks, the impress, as it were, of their author. I do not think that a soul can be deceived, provided it is humble and simple and that it does not desire to be deceived. It is sufficient for a person to have only once seen our Lord, to be perfectly able to recognise a vision caused by the devil. The latter may begin by causing a certain kind of pleasure, but it will be in vain, as the soul rejects it with a sort of instinctive horror. It sees that the love which is offered it, is not chaste and pure, and the enemy is soon detected and exposed. Therefore, I say that the devil cannot injure a soul that is at all experienced."

[1] Her life, p. 312.

In place of devils, let us take, if you will, an influence caused by disease, but even in cases of this sort,[1] which are of a purely psychological nature, neither St Theresa, nor the saints who have resembled her, allow themselves to be duped. Hysterical suggestion, so like in appearance to demoniacal, is perfectly well-known to them. They have watched its approach, recognised it and vigorously repelled it, and they have been rewarded for their energetic action, by the triumph, in them, of a spirit which has absolutely nothing in common with the former spirit.

The intellectual characteristics of this latter spirit are, in the first place, very different from those of the former, for its inspirations are recognised by the subject, who reasons about them, consents to them, and in a certain sense, wills them. In nervous patients, suggestion, like hallucination, is depressing, disorganising and sterile. In order to prove that such were not the effects of the stigmata of St Francis of Assisi, the revelations of St Theresa or the visions of Blessed Margaret Mary, it will not be necessary even to point to the marvellous fecundity of their spiritual creations, still less to enter into an argu-

[1] According to P. Bonniot, the two states resemble one another pretty closely, and we may therefore (for the time being, at least) carry on the discussion on purely psychological lines. "In the one case," he says, "the devil acts upon the subject, in the other, the experimenter, and this is about the only difference between the two cases." "In like manner," he adds, "possessions are cases of hypnotism, in which the evil spirit plays the part of hypnotiser." I do not know whether this opinion is approved of and final, but it is, in any case, most interesting and plausible.

ment with those who deny that religion, rightly understood and practised, is the greatest power humanity has at its disposal. St Theresa herself, with her wonderful insight and her still more wonderful common sense, comes to our assistance with a far more practical line of reasoning.

When first she began her method of prayer, she found it a hard struggle to persevere; "I own,"[1] she says, "that many a time I should have preferred the hardest penance to the torment of having to recollect myself in prayer. I made efforts against myself, however, and God helped me. But in order to conquer myself I had to make use of all the courage I possess, which is not slight, so I am told."

This trial of her courage did not soon end. "Such,"[2] she says, "is our melancholy condition on this earth. As long as our poor soul remains united to this mortal body, it is a prisoner and shares the infirmities of the body. It is affected by the weather and by variations of health, and it often finds itself, without any fault on its part, incapable of doing what it would like to do. Forcing only aggravates and prolongs the evil. Such persons ought to understand that they are ill."

But does she take pleasure in this state of depression, as she calls it? Is she going to let herself fall into a state of complete prostration, of deadly ennui, distaste for life, discouragement, fear and utter despair, which, according to doctors, is the fate of hysterical subjects?[3] Hardly; for listen to the advice

---

[1] Her life, p. 85.   [2] Her life, p. 114.
[3] Pierre Janet. See work quoted above.

—and the example—she gives to persons who find themselves in a like condition to hers. "A soul, however weak it may be, can always find occupation in useful reading and works of charity." "Let them seek recreation in holy conversation or go and breathe country air. . One can always serve God, no matter what condition one may be in. His yoke is light, and it is of the greatest importance that the soul should not remain depressed or sad. It should be led gently for its greater spiritual profit."

The saint therefore goes on her way with renewed courage. Her body may indeed resist and even break down, but when reminded of her state of health she replies, "What would it matter even if I did die!" "As a matter of fact," she tells us, "I have felt much better since I began to treat myself with less care and delicacy."[1] All this sounds extremely unlike the hysterical patient who, though perfectly able to walk, eat, and lift weights, imagines that he can do none of these things. It is an exactly opposite state of affairs. If the saint listened only to the dictates of nature, she would remain inactive, incapacitated by the nervous spasms which shake her whole being, crippled by infirmities or fever, checked on all sides by violent antipathies, and lost in the flood of wild and useless explanations which her wayward imagination would be for ever suggesting to her. But, on the contrary, she works on, and without relying too much upon the marvellous cures she from time to time obtains for herself and others, she insists that suffering nature should contribute the amount and,

[1] Her life, p. 126, *cf.* p. 177.

what is more, the right quality of work which duty requires. In her case, as in others, the imagination may indeed act like a regular mill-clapper, "ever revolving and noisy," to use her own expression, but she does not waste time idly listening to it, and neglecting "to make the flour." She may have trials but she is not led astray by them. She grinds the corn the best way she can, trusting to God to come to her assistance if she does her part and to enable her to draw, not only merit, but increased moral strength from this state of things.

The will, which in hysterical subjects is so paralysed, in her case unites itself even more closely to God than the intelligence and the memory. "It is not a spiritual sleep," she tells us, "but the will acts alone." While the other faculties yield to nature, the will secures for them a safe refuge in God, to which, as the saint puts it so prettily, they can return "like doves, which, misliking the food they seek first on one side and then on the other, hasten, after a fruitless search, to return to the dovecot." Elsewhere she compares the firm, patient will, to the prudent bee which remains in the hive in order to extract honey from the flowers which its companions bring it (sic). "For if, instead of staying in the hive, all the bees went out one after the other, how could the honey be made?"[1]

It is clear, therefore, that great saints may experience phenomena of a pathological nature, which a doctor of nervous diseases is sorely tempted to consider his property. How is it that they contrive

[1] Her life, p. 138, 149.

to get the better of such incidental symptoms? Do these yield at last to the influence of the healthy parts of their organisation? Possibly; but the victory is due far more to the strong attachment of the will to duty, to habits of self-control, and to the good use they make of each painful and humiliating occurrence. Temperament and character are, in this way, modified. "Naturally," St Theresa tells us, "whatever I desired, I desired with impetuosity, but now God so calms my aspirations that when I obtain what I desire, I hardly feel any joy at all. After passing through the most terrible crises, which she describes with great fidelity and minuteness of detail, she is more and more confirmed in a state of mind so utterly unlike hysteria in its effects, as to be, apparently, its exact opposite.

Is it true to say that the spiritual states of the saints cause "a narrowing of the field of consciousness"? Those who take account only of those things which fill up three parts of the daily lives of the majority of men, will unhesitatingly reply in the affirmative. Does not the soul of the saint gradually withdraw itself from all that interests and touches us? Is there not a "daily increase in the number of things which it ceases to think about? Are not many of the saints to be rightly compared to the occupants of a house, the doors and windows of which are closed up one after the other, in order that those inside may be compelled to think only of heavenly things?"

Before this argument can be of any psychological value, we must first prove that, in the mind of the mystic, the ideas which he discards are not replaced

EXTRAORDINARY PHENOMENA 115

by any other ideas, that the interior life is more empty and ideas suggested by the thought of the next world are more barren of results, than are the lives of the worldly and the ideas which this world suggests. Next, tha desires for the glory of God and the conversion of sinners, the direction of souls, the foundation of an order, the care of a church, and still more the reform of the Church Universal, do not call for anything like the sustained energy that is needed by men who seek only for fame and amusement.

Lastly, in lives such as these, is there a "division of the personality"? Some will say that there is, and in proof they will instance those raptures after which the soul, unable by its own strength to sustain itself at such a height, falls back to earth. But in these cases, there is no sign of the "division" which reveals the presence of hysteria. Few souls have been so possessed by the love of God as St Catherine of Genoa, and few have passed through such a martyrdom of soul and body as she had to endure. And yet, her biographer tells us that "she did not omit to perform punctually all the duties which are a necessary part of ordinary life." And again: "She had a husband whose character was strange and irregular, and who caused her to suffer great misery, but God enabled her to endure everything without complaint, silently and with extreme patience." How, we may ask, can these two sorts of lives possibly combine and exist side by side? And yet they do, and their combination is the special work accomplished by sanctity. St Catherine of Genoa combined them so successfully in herself that she persevered in asking and finally obtained the conversion of her husband.

All the saints, without exception, even those of their number who were most inclined to mysticism, agree in teaching that the roughest employments and the humblest and most repulsive offices should be the chosen lot of those who are favoured by visions and ecstasies. Far from supplanting and ignoring one another, these two existences are fed and strengthened by contact with one another. According to St Theresa, Martha and Mary do not try each to supplant the other in the soul of the saint, for "the soul knows very well that it ought not to desire to be Mary till it has laboured with Martha."[1] Even when it has been raised to the state of Mary, "it is able, at the same time, to fill the office of Martha. In this way, it combines the active and the contemplative life, and while remaining united to God, it is able to employ itself in works of charity, in reading, and the duties of its state of life." When the saint had finally attained to the highest degree of union with God, she was far from feeling herself less able to return to the things of earth. She compared herself to a bird which, when its wings have become strong enough to fly to greater heights, is also better able to descend quickly and safely. "Everything helped me to know God better and to love Him better than ever before."

We have now pursued this comparison long enough, and it has, I trust, enabled us to recognise

[1] St Theresa. Her life, p. 230, *cf.* p. 166, 222.

some of the most wonderful characteristics of the saints.

Unlike nervous diseases, sanctity is not a "disintegration" of the powers of the mind; it is an "aggregation" of the closest possible kind, which derives its strength from a higher principle, under the control of which it forms and sustains itself.

It is not a "narrowing of the field of consciousness," but rather the opening-out of a wider field, although it is true that this opening-out is at the cost, if we may use the expression, of a narrowing of the field of passing sensations and empty illusions.

Neither is it a "division of the personality," although it certainly creates a new personality, and that at the cost of great sacrifice and much suffering. This new personality is not a medley of divided and disordered parts. It exhibits a cohesion, a strength and a unity above anything else which psychology can shew us. This new personality also retains whatever was best of the original personality, and these surviving elements combine peacefully with the new.

The truth of the above statements will be clearly shewn when we come to study more in detail and with greater precision, the various qualities of the saints, their understanding, their love and their aptitude for active work.

CHAPTER IV

THE SENSES AND THE IMAGINATION. THE UNDERSTANDING AND CONTEMPLATION

FROM the extraordinary phenomena in the saint's life, we now pass on to consider the more hidden course of his existence, his daily trials and his unceasing efforts. In so doing, we shall not, as it were, descend the stream; on the contrary, we shall ascend to a source which tradition has ever taught us to hold sacred.

The saint is a man of God and we must not be surprised, therefore, to find that his faculties are put to very hard work indeed, in order that everything that impedes the service of God may be eliminated and all that leads to and facilitates that service may be increased and strengthened. The saints tell us so themselves, over and over again. It is no exaggeration to say that their ideas on the nature of the soul and on the harmony between its faculties, constitute a complete psychology of the saints. This theoretical psychology, of which their writings are full, throws a valuable light upon the practical psychology of their lives.

Of ecclesiastical teachers, St Augustine was the first to divide the powers of the soul into three: the memory, the understanding, and the will, and this division has been a familiar one to all those who have come after him. It is referred to at every turn by St Catherine of Siena, St Theresa, St John of the Cross, and St Ignatius.

"His life is well-regulated," says St Catherine of Siena,[1] "because he has regulated the three powers of his soul: the memory retains the recollection of the benefits he has received from God; the understanding strives to know His will; and the will, to love Him." "In this," she tells us elsewhere, "consists all well-regulated life, both of soul and body, in every place and circumstance in which we may find ourselves. The powers of the soul must act in concert: the memory must recall the thought of God's benefits; the understanding must strive to know His will, and the will must love Him to such a degree that it is unable to love or desire anything apart from Him."

In like manner, St Ignatius insists, in his first "Exercise," that we should meditate on the first sin, the sin of the rebel angels. This exercise he divides into three parts: the exercise of the memory to recall the sin; the exercise of the understanding to "reflect upon it in greater detail," and the exercise of the will "to excite the consequent affections of the soul."

This threefold division is, of course, susceptible of further subdivision, and it is far from necessarily excluding those, for instance, which deal with the great complexity of the will, or which distinguish between the imagination and the memory, and so on. Those who hold to it, do not, however, appear to take very great account of the influence of the senses and

[1] See "Letters," I. 261, 367.

of those exterior impressions, which, according to modern ideas, are the source of all consciousness and of all knowledge. With the saints, sentiment is not a separate faculty, nor do they associate love with that passive and emotional sentiment, which gains in interest among our contemporaries in proportion as it shews itself the more ill-regulated and diseased. According to them, the will is no arbitrary and negative force, and in placing it, as they do, in such intimate relation with love, they wish to point out that there is its mainstay and the source of all its strength;—its mainstay, because, in their eyes, a will that does not love or that does not love the object most worthy of love, is a dead force,—the source of its strength—because the love by which it is upheld is stronger than death. In short, in their brief but precise theories, the most prominent place is given to the will, upheld by love and enlightened by an understanding, which we must not be surprised to find cares more for fidelity than originality.

All said and done, however, everything must begin at the senses and at the imagination which preserves, continues, renews and diversifies the impressions conveyed by means of them. Is the saint a man who despises imagination and labours to destroy it, or, on the contrary, does he cultivate and make use of it? Allowances must first be made, for the natural temperament of the saint, for his social surroundings and the kind of study by which he has developed his mind. It is not surprising to find that St Jerome, St Francis of Assisi, St Theresa and St Francis of Sales were by nature

THE SENSES AND THE IMAGINATION 121

possessed of a far livelier imagination than St Thomas Aquinas, St Jane de Chantal and M. Olier. When this much has been granted, there still remains the fact that the particular character of Catholic dogma and morality, the study of Scripture, the teaching of certain recognised spiritual works (for instance, *The Imitation*), meditation, solitude, community life and finally, tradition, must exercise a lasting influence upon the cast of mind of great mystics, a class to which, as we have seen, all the saints belong.

The following passage is taken from the writings of one of those contemporary philosophers who are either genuinely interested in the psychology of the saints or who fancy themselves to be so: " Love, ecstasy, desire for perfection, the tendency to materialise and to represent the Deity in concrete form, such are the essential characteristics of mysticism."[1] A set of incongruous elements certainly, and, to say the least, of very unequal importance. Love, undoubtedly, is an element of mysticism, and desire of perfection follows upon it. Ecstasy is, as we have seen, a less common ingredient, and as for the tendency to materialise, we are somewhat surprised to find it associated with mysticism, the opposite word "spirituality" being so very often used of the aspirations and habits of mind of mystics. It will be of interest to determine which of these two contradictory expressions is the right one.

As a rule, the saints do not despise any of God's

[1] Paulhan. *Les Caractères.* Paris: Alcan.

gifts—"Let each one give us the benefit of her intelligence to-day," St Theresa once said to her nuns at recreation. "*No one has too much.*" Quite true, no one has too much, and the difficulty lies rather in making a good use of what we have. The imagination is especially liable to condemnation, if on account of it we turn away from God, and become attached to this earth. It then causes us to anticipate, prolong and revel in the pleasures of the senses, while in every aspect of nature it affords us a foretaste or aftertaste of delights we either desire or regret. This evil is too obvious for it to be necessary that I should dwell upon it here.

Again, the saints hold that the imagination is dangerous when, under pretext of drawing the soul into the ways of God and of His love, it represents Him under a form which is unworthy of Him. But are not all sensible forms unworthy of the Divinity? Absolutely speaking they are, and none realise this fact better than the saints themselves. According to them there are two reasons why we should watch carefully over the pleasure we feel in forms which take hold of the imagination. To begin with, there is danger of the illusion which mistakes the echo of voices, proceeding from these inner depths where pride and sensuality thrive almost unsuspected by the soul, which is a prey to them, for heavenly inspirations. After countless experiences, a St Theresa may end by distinguishing clearly when the soul is speaking and when it is listening, but it will cost, even one like her, not a little to get as far as this. Therefore it is that

St John of the Cross is so careful to warn souls against the temptation of thinking that they are listening when, in reality, they are only talking to themselves. " There are persons," he says, " scarcely able to meditate, who, when they hear certain interior words, fancy that these must proceed from God. Their love of listening to these words and the desire they have of hearing them, makes them answer themselves, and then they persuade themselves that these answers come from God. These persons fall into great absurdities."[1]

Another extreme, which the saints are careful to guard against, is that of identifying the action of God with these sensible phenomena, and of thinking that such phenomena are infallible signs of the union of the soul with God. " All the images of the imagination," says St John of the Cross, " are confined within very narrow limits; and the Divine Wisdom, to which the understanding ought to unite itself, is infinite, absolutely pure and absolutely simple, and it is not confined within the limits of any distinct, particular or finite mind. The soul which desires to unite itself to the Divine Wisdom must necessarily bear some proportion and likeness to it, and consequently it must shake itself free from the images of the imagination which would give it limits. It must not attach itself to any particular form of thought, but it must be pure, simple, without limits or material ideas, in order to approach, in some degree, to God, who cannot be expressed by any bodily likeness, or by any single finite conception."

[1] Work already quoted, p. 131, *cf.* p. 82.

Here, certainly, we find a saint whose mysticism does not consist in "materialising" or in "representing God under a concrete form." And we may be equally sure that his doctrine (based as it is, on personal experience) is that of all the saints. When the author of the above fanciful theory set to work to seek for examples, he fell in with the life of Blessed Maria of Agreda, and he was obliged, in spite of his theory, to admit that whenever she felt that her visions and communications came through the senses and imagination, whose effects she recognised in herself, she at once turned away from them and "placed herself in a state of indifference." She would not allow the animal and sensitive part to enjoy the sweet fruits of God's mercy, but endeavoured to leave it unsatisfied.[1] If carefully read, the works of St Theresa, St Catherine of Genoa, and those like them, will be found to contain similar declarations at every turn.

Are we therefore to understand that the saints have succeeded in getting rid of every material representation which either preceded or followed the visions they were sometimes favoured with? This was the contention of the quietists. One of the errors contained in their theories and condemned by the Church consisted in banishing from mental prayer all recollection of the Sacred Humanity which they held to be an obstacle to perfect contemplation. No saint ever carried his spirituality as far as this: the distinction between God, con-

[1] Paulhan, work already quoted, p. 191.

THE SENSES AND THE IMAGINATION 125

sidered in His eternal essence and God, known in the mystery of the Incarnation, being the very basis of Christianity. St Theresa, who not only practically experienced, but who also understood and explained the profoundest depths of the life of sanctity, speaks, in regard to this matter, with her usual sound good sense.

"It is doubtless a good thing," she says, "to set aside material imaginings, since spiritual persons say that it is so, but, in my opinion, this should not be attempted before the soul is very far advanced, as it is clear, that till then, it ought to seek the Creator by means of creatures."[1] "To do otherwise," she continues, anticipating Pascal, "is to act as if we were angels." For this reason, she recommends the sensible devotions practised by so many saints before her time: devotions to the infancy of our Lord, to His wounds, His cross, and His blood; for what is a "devotion" in reality but a reasoned application of the imagination and the mind to one of the mysteries which the believing soul desires to contemplate and meditate?

Next to Christ, the imagination of the saints loves to picture the sufferings, trials, consolations, and triumphs of other saints, and to dwell upon the ceremonies by which they are commemorated, and the feasts by which their virtues are honoured and symbolised.

Every event in history, every aspect of nature, and above all, every miracle, reminds them of the power of God, and these are so many steps by which

[1] Her life, p. 229.

their human weakness is enabled to raise itself by degrees to the eternal essence of the pure spirit.

When once the imagination has consented to let itself be purified and directed, sanctity allows it flight enough to satisfy the most ardent natures and the most enamoured of this world's delights. Now, it is the infancy of Christ which, placed before its eyes, shews it all the freshness of an age which personifies innocence, weakness, and hope. Now it can join with St Francis of Assisi as he sings his Canticle of the Sun, and now again in the Canticle of Canticles it can enjoy all the poetry and make its own all those daring comparisons and those aspirations of the soul towards God, those tender dialogues and burning allegories and descriptions, which to the superficial or prejudiced mind do but suggest a revolt on the part of unrestrained sensual passion.

With St Gertrude this loving effusion becomes a sort of symphony in which all the senses take a share. In her aspirations towards God, she appears, as it were, inebriated by perfumes, spiritual potions, gentle sounds and harmonies. But this apparent indulgence of the senses leaves intact everything that could be required by the purest metaphysics and the most patient and disinterested charity. Thus, both those who speak of a tendency to materialise and those who see nothing but spirituality in mysticism are in one sense wrong, and in another, right. The saint, undoubtedly, spiritualises whatever comes to him through the senses and imagination, just as he strives to bring his nature into touch with truth.

With less freedom and charm than we find in St Francis of Assisi, St Gertrude, St Theresa, and St Francis of Sales, for there is more " method " about him, St Ignatius of Loyola is careful to tell us (Second Week) that it is a useful thing to exercise the five senses of the imagination. " I will see with the eyes of the imagination; I will hear with the help of the imagination ; I will taste with the help of the imagination.   ."

One and all of these saints, therefore, despite the diversity of their temperaments, held firmly both to the doctrine of the Incarnation and to those portions of peripatetic philosophy which have been incorporated into thomistic theology.[1]

Here, as elsewhere, we must distinguish between various phases in the spiritual life of the saints. The mystic dies and is born again. He dies to a sensual, agitated, troubled world, liable to corruption and destined to perish, and is born again to a transformed world. To quote his own expression, he passes through the night of the senses, after which his purified eyes are opened to a more brilliant light. This is substantially the allegory of the cave,—that sublime portion of platonic metaphysics in which the purification of the senses is required as a preparation for the illumination of the mind. What is of importance to notice is that the saint will return, later on, to sensible objects, to enjoy them, in his own way, of course, but far more intensely

[1] See Appendix.

than other men. He will return with all the greater alacrity, as the senses to which these objects appeal, though formerly stained and disordered, were so, not through their own fault or that of the objects themselves, but through the fault of the mind. "It is in the mind," says St John of the Cross, "that the disorders of the animal part of our nature take rise, and from it that they derive their strength."[1]

The purification of the senses is accomplished by means of the purification of the mind. When the mind is healed, the senses which are animated by it are deprived of their poison. We have just seen that St Theresa taught that we ought first to seek the Creator in creatures. She also tells us that when once we have advanced far enough in perfection we shall be able to return to creatures through the Creator, and that we shall then find them pure and adorned with the beauty they possessed in days of primeval innocence. Her great friend, St John of the Cross, expressed the same idea in more abstract language:

"God certainly does not wish to destroy nature; on the contrary he wishes to perfect it." "The soul (when united to God) falls at first into a state of great forgetfulness. With regard to exterior things, it then shews so great a negligence and so great a contempt of self that, lost in God, it forgets to eat or drink, and it no longer knows if it has done a thing or not, or whether or not it has been spoken to by anyone. . But once the soul has become firmly established in the habit of a union, which is its

---

[1] St John of the Cross, Work quoted above, p. 282.

sovereign good, it no longer forgets reasonable things, and things of moral and physical necessity.—On the contrary, it is more perfect when engaged in works suitable to its state of life, although it accomplishes them by the help of images and knowledge which God excites in a special manner in the memory. All the powers of the soul are, as it were, transformed in God." [1]

From the imagination and memory we naturally pass on to consider the intellect or the understanding properly so called.

We must not expect too many miracles from God. Sanctity may create an equality in love and devotedness among souls, but it does not effect a similar transformation among minds. To the end St Paul's brain remained vastly superior to that of St Peter, and yet who can tell which of these two saints approached nearer to the Source of all light and truth? And in like manner, the least among the companions of St Francis Xavier may have possessed a martyr's courage fully equal to his, but for all that God was in no way bound to bestow upon him a gift for the direction of souls such as the saint enjoyed, any more than He is obliged to endow all simple and pious monks with the metaphysical genius of St Augustine and St Thomas or the creative genius of St Vincent of Paul.

The understanding, therefore, is a faculty which naturally varies greatly in quality among the saints. Some saints have been comparatively simple-minded,

[1] Work cited above, p. 146.

and, humanly speaking, very ignorant. It is the sight of such as these, that creates the idea in many people's minds that in the Church sanctity is inseparably allied with a degree of mortification calculated to restrain and stifle the gifts of nature. Those of the saints who are credited with the possession of genius are set down as persons whose faith made them blindly obedient, and who became saints by sacrificing their natural gifts and thus reducing themselves by artificial means to the same humble condition in which the rest were born and in which they lived all their lives. This is an absolutely mistaken idea. Ignorance had no more to do with the sanctity of the youthful martyr than genius had with the sanctity of St Thomas. The psychology of the saints does not undertake, therefore, to make a correct estimate of the degree of intelligence possessed by one or other of the souls of the Blessed; its object is rather to show how they used their minds, whether great or small, and how these latter developed under the influence of sanctity.

The saints distrust no kind of knowledge or science in itself. As far as they are personally concerned, they prefer the life of Christ and of the Church as a subject of meditation, to the life of plants and animals, or the constitution of minerals. But in other people, or when required by their own vocation in life to take up secular study, they despise no kind of work or department of knowledge, for everything has been made by God and everything therefore can be studied with a view to His glory.

What the saints lay most stress upon with regard to science, is the spirit in which men seek to acquire and to teach it. Bossuet's well-known saying puts their case in a nutshell—" Woe to that science that does not teach us to love." By love he means action, action for the glory of God, for justice, and for the relief of human misery. The saints condemn vainglorious science, for the vainglorious man never loves. They also blame rash science, for rashness is a form of pride. But when science is neither rash nor vainglorious, the saints are keenly alive to its merits, for they know that love and action require to be directed by knowledge. The Gospel tells us not to hide our light under a bushel, and St Paul entreats his disciples: " This I pray you, that your charity may more and more abound in knowledge and in all understanding: that you may approve the better things."[1] These words are often forgotten by imprudent or idle souls, but a St Vincent of Paul remembers them. It is he who has taught us to substitute forethought and organised charity for charity which is impulsive, unreflecting, and unmethodical.

The saint, no doubt, is often a man of intuitive perception. He was either born so or he has become so, and it is customary to declare that flashes of illuminating grace come upon him which take the place of reflection and spare him the trouble of thinking. I do not deny that inspirations may come to him, and I do not care to know whether intuitive minds, which jump to sudden conclusions, as distinguished from patient and reflective minds, are more frequent among saints than among other men.

[1] Phil. i. 9-10.

There are quite sufficient well-known cases of saints who certainly hesitated and took time to make up their minds. The saint who spends many days in examining his own conscience—and in getting others to examine theirs—does not think it necessary to keep the whole world informed of his experiences and methods of reasoning. Every now and then some maxim or a few pregnant words escape him, in spite of his humility and love of silence, which give us some idea of the store he must have laid up of thoughts and recollections.

Abbé le Monnier is right when he says that a whole educational treatise is contained in the seven words of St Francis of Assisi to Brother Elias: " Watch, warn, labour, nourish, love, wait, fear." [1]

We may take it for granted that this power of conveying great truths in very few words was not possessed by the saint at the very outset of his career, but that it was the result of a lifetime of patient labour and of much sowing, cultivating, and reaping, both in his own soul and in the souls of others.

And yet, someone may object, the saint is not troubled by doubts. If by doubts is meant doubts about faith, I agree; but if it is suggested that the saint goes straight ahead, looking neither to the right nor the left, in blind response to every inspiration that happens to seize him,—this, I say, is absolutely untrue.

In order to see this, we have only to compare the

[1] The Latin is still more expressive: *Vigila, admone, labora, pasce, ama, expecta, time.*

sceptic and the believer. The real sceptic believes neither in a dispensing Providence, nor in a pre-established order of things, nor in immutable laws. He denies that either conviction or virtue rests upon solid foundations. In his opinion, therefore, nothing is impossible. His own desires and wayward imagination lead him to hope for everything, and, given the circumstances, there is nothing he does not attempt to prove, and, as a last resort, affirm to be true. He is as little influenced by objections as he is deterred by scruples. It is no paradox, therefore, to describe the sceptic as a man who believes everything.

The believer, on the other hand, knows that he has to reckon with certain things. He knows the ground he is standing on, but he is also aware that he is surrounded by a good deal else which he cannot master, and which resists his best attempts at investigation. The more certain he is that there is an established order of things, both solid and fruitful, the more clearly he perceives an almost infinite vista of untold possibilities. He knows that to deal with them would be a matter of extreme difficulty to a mere isolated passer-by—such as he is, in this world —and, therefore, he makes up his mind to doubt until he is certain that a fact bears the impress of truth upon it.[1]

The saint has a firmer hold on the truths of faith

---

[1] St Catherine of Siena makes the following curious remark in a letter to Queen Joan of Naples: "If you say: I still doubt: at least remain neutral until you see clearly. . . Seek explanations and counsel from those whom you know for certain fear God" (Letters, I. 218).

than even the ordinary believer, but he is, therefore, all the more distrustful of the promptings of an understanding that is imprudent, hasty, prejudiced, and egotistical. The intellectual life of most saints is a wonderfully interesting mixture of liberty—one might almost say audacity—combined with a craving for order and unity. Most people imagine that in the Catholic Church this craving, which nothing short of submission can satisfy, crushes the life out of every other aspiration; but, as a matter of fact, we do not find that this is the case with the most highly favoured of her children. The saints certainly desire unity, and if absolute silence were necessary in order to attain to it, silent they would willingly become; and if the sacrifice of their lives were needed, they would gladly give them up. But if speaking will help, they speak; and if, instead of giving way to others, they believe that they can, and in the interests of truth ought to, make others yield to them, they spend all their time, trouble, and prayer to gain this latter end. Whatever doubts were at first raised by prudence and humble self-diffidence, vanish, and give place to faith which is not only courageous but "violent," as the Gospel tells us it ought to be.

St Paul wished at any cost to agree with St Peter, but when he saw that he erred in adopting a line of action, calculated to impede the conversion of the Gentiles, he reproved him publicly, and, what is more, gained him over to his own way of thinking. St Bernard, St Catherine of Siena, and many another saint, has acted in like manner with regard to the popes. The Gospel says that St John outran St Peter, and came first to the Sepulchre and looked in, but that he would not be the first to enter. Theologians say that his action was symbolical of what habitually takes place in the Church. All great saints, whether founders or reformers, were in advance of the pope of their day. They did not wait to take the initiative from him. What they expected of him was final recognition and permission to extend their work throughout the universal Church.

Some one or more of my readers may perhaps be astonished at what I am now going to say. It is commonly supposed that, in the Church, all original views, bold innovations, fruitful inventions, or interest in intellectual problems, have emanated from heresiarchs, while the saints, having done violence to themselves in order to continue obedient to authority, remain stationary and opposed to all such things. Nothing can be further from the truth. Were it not that the word *heresiarch* has come to bear a very sinister meaning, we should be perfectly justified in maintaining that the greatest heresiarchs, that is to say, the boldest innovators, the most eager searchers after truths—not new in themselves, perhaps, and in so far as they touch upon dogma, but new at any rate to the generation which hears them —are the saints. Does not the Church derive the very form of her teaching from the teaching of her doctors, and is it not as true to say that the saints make the Church as to say that the Church makes and sanctifies the saints? In what then do heresiarchs[1] (according to the sense now attached to the word) differ from saints? In this, that the former suppress, cut down, narrow, and impoverish; their famous so-called "choice" of which they are so proud consisting always in an exclusion, either of grace to the seeming gain of liberty, or of liberty for the sake of an apparent glorification of grace alone —in a suppression, that is to say, of one or other of the two natures in Christ, etc. The saint, on his side, makes choice of a truth which he then develops, of a need of mankind or of the Church which he intends to supply, or of a charitable work which he wishes to begin; but in the process of development he destroys nothing, on the contrary, he causes one more shoot to bud forth from the everlasting Tree.

We have seen that while they use their minds, the saints do not omit to pray a great deal. This seems rather an obvious remark to make, but still we may ask, why exactly do they pray? Do they wish to obtain a revelation which will enable them to dispense with reflection and thought? Yet when these revelations are granted (which would seem to be

---

[1] The word "heresy" is now only used in an opprobrious sense, but formerly it signified nothing more than a choice, a party, or sect which might be either good or bad. This is the meaning of the Greek αἱρεσις derived from αἱροῦμαι, I take, I choose, I adhere to. The philosophers gave the name of *Christian heresy* to the religion of Jesus Christ. St Paul says that, as a Jew, he followed the "*heresy of the Pharisees*," the most esteemed of any among the Jews. If heresy had meant error in those days, the name would have been more properly applied to the sect of the Sadducees than to that of the Pharisees.—Bergier: *Dict. of Theology.*

seldom enough) they appear to inaugurate rather than end a period of anxiety and struggle for the saint. The saints seem to pray chiefly in order to rid their minds of everything that by running counter to two or three essential predominant ideas would serve to confuse, darken, and mislead them.[1]

They aim at possessing that single eye spoken of in the Gospel—the word single here signifies purified. Purified therefore of what? Of those causes of error which logicians so carefully analyse.[2] What we want is not so much to multiply demonstrations as to clear away from before our eyes those veils which are spread by want of simplicity, by anxiety, exaggeration, obstinacy, self-love—in a word, by passion. The false mystic delights in analysing his own personal aspirations, and in subtleties and mysteries. The true mystic asks for light, and chiefly for light to recognise the necessity of sacrifice.

I drew attention above to the contrast which exists, up to a certain point, between Bossuet's ideas and those of M. Olier. On this particular point, I find that they are entirely of one mind in the common-sense view they take of the matter. Bossuet applies to the saints our Lord's words to His Father as given by St John: "The glory which Thou hast given me, I have given to them" (St John xvii. 22). He understands sanctity to be light—given and re-

---

[1] The Scriptures tell us that "the soul of a holy man discovereth sometimes true things more than seven watchmen that sit in a high place to watch" (Eccl. xxxvii. 18).

[2] See Appendix.

ceived. M. Olier, on his side, dwells on the inner meaning of this idea when he tells one of his friends[1] not to allow his mind to be "perplexed" by the new opinions (he is particularly referring to the Jansenists), which will cause him to lose "clearness of mind": "I pray our Lord to preserve it to you, as it is one of the things most essential to perfect sanctity. Clear light is a privilege reserved for heaven and for those solitary souls whom God has delivered from the world and its darkness. I beg of you not to let your mind be troubled." He ends with a few words which certainly justify me in what I said above of his respect for common sense: "Do not strive after high and extraordinary perfection."[2]

This simplicity which seeks nothing underhand or exceptional, which is guilty of no evasions but goes straight to the point, is not only good for those who, by their condition in life, and tastes, or rather vocation, are far removed from scientific interests. It is quite as precious a boon to those who cultivate science, and they feel the need of it so keenly that when first they start on the road to sanctity, they seek it to the exclusion of all else. In his youth, St Philip Neri, the future founder of the Italian oratory, sold his books and gave the price to the poor. So did St Dominic. The latest biographer of St Philip[3] is, however, obliged to add that "later on he will return to his books and will no longer fear to combine his

[1] Letters, I., p. 464.
[2] This remark must be taken *cum grano salis*. I do not suppose it needs any further explanation.
[3] See *Saint Philippe de Néri* by Countess d'Estienne. Paris: Lecoffre.

acquired sacred science with all that is best in human learning." Many other saints have done as he did. In their first fervour they discarded the written for the living book, learning the secrets of the spiritual life by means of detachment, humility, and action, and only returning to science when their will and their love had grown strong. For then they were able to recognise the truth of St Theresa's words: " Piety without science may fill souls with illusions and inspire them with a taste for childish and silly devotions." Therefore this saint loved " men who were distinguished by learning," and she warned souls against men who were only half-educated as likely to their harm. She adds, " I have found that, provided they are men of good morals, they are better with no learning at all than with only a little, for in the former case, at least, they do not trust to their own lights but take counsel of really enlightened persons."

The saints also frequently experienced the need of a division of labour such as is required by difference of condition, sex, vocation and aptitude. Everyone is not equal to carrying out the magnificent programme laid down by Bossuet for the oratorians:—"To devote themselves to the reading of the Scriptures so that they may acquire the letter of it by study, the spirit of it by prayer, its inner meaning by solitude, its healing power by practice, its end by charity, which is the goal of all things." But what one saint cannot do alone, many may accomplish together for the good of all, and to the profit of each one individually. If it is true that the religious orders have produced more saints than life in the world,[1] one, at least, of the reasons is here set before us.

We should be passing over a considerable portion of the lives of our saints if we were to leave unnoticed two apparently contradictory states which are experienced by the greater number of them. I mean, on the one hand, their spirit of reflection and their habits of self-interrogation and self-judgment, and on the other hand, their self-abandonment to that so-called passive prayer in which they seem to aspire not so much to perfection as to a suspension of the operations of reason.

Both these states are known to be of importance in the life of the mystic, and they have provoked endless discussion as much, and rightly, on theological as on psychological grounds. It is extremely difficult to gain a proper understanding of the different aspects under which the saint's faculties display themselves.

Do the saints believe themselves to be forbidden to study or reflect? The question sounds a strange one in the case of a religion which insists upon meditation and still more upon confession preceded by examination of conscience. But truth, which is ever simple in itself, has, in this instance as in many another, been strangely distorted. It will help us to restore things to their right place if we read over the two following articles of the Conference of Issy, written out by Bossuet:—

"XVI. Reflections upon ourselves, our actions and

[1] See Appendix.

the gifts we have received, which we see everywhere practised by the prophets and apostles, for the purpose of giving thanks to God for His benefits and for other similar ends, are of use to all the faithful and even to the most perfect souls. The doctrine which tends to discourage this practice is erroneous and nearly allied to heresy.

"XVII. No reflections are dangerous and bad, excepting those which cause us to look back upon our actions and upon the gifts we have received with a view to feeding our self-love, to finding support in nature, or to becoming immersed in ourselves."

This is the twofold conviction of the saints. They are careful to examine themselves and why? In order to discern by what spirit they are led and to find out how far they correspond with grace and how much share sensuality and self-love have in the torments and the delights which agitate their souls. Instead of avoiding self-knowledge and hiding what they are from themselves, they look their gifts in the face, and I do not say always, but at any rate frequently, they gather from the sight an involuntary conviction of their own sanctity.

And is this conviction incompatible with that humility which is the groundwork of Christian sanctity? No; and this is one of the most interesting—I might almost say dramatic—incidents in the spiritual lives of the saints. We have seen the doubts which assailed St Bernard on the score of his miracles. More than one of his fellow-saints experienced the same, and more than one has been obliged to yield to the evidence before his eyes, and recognise with gratitude the gifts by means of which God raised him to sanctity. St Francis of Sales owned to Mme. de Chantal that his canonisation was not impossible, and St Vincent of Paul not only foretold his own canonisation but informed the future Pope Calixtus III. that he would have to pronounce the decree.

These, and such-like instances, have caused a certain psychologist to remark that "pride and humility thrive apace in the souls of the saints." As well say they put out an eye in order to see better, for these two qualities are absolutely incompatible one with the other. No; the saints do not combine pride with humility.—They combine personal humility with a clear knowledge of all that God has done for them (*fecit mihi magna qui potens est*). It was not pride that made St Paul write as he did. "I am the least of the apostles, who am not worthy to be called an apostle... But by the grace of God I am what I am; and His grace in me hath not been void" (1 Cor. xv. 9, 10). Elsewhere he says, with a magnificent simplicity, "Be ye followers of me as I also am of Christ" (*Ibid.*, iv. 16 and xi. 1). Many saints have imitated him in describing the wonders God worked in their souls. St Catherine of Siena felt compelled to describe her visions to her confessor, in order that he might judge of her sins in the light of the graces she had received. St Theresa did the same, and we are, therefore, able to understand the otherwise surprising degree of remorse she felt and the accusations of infidelity she so constantly brought against herself. The saints realise both the gifts they have received and the obligations these entail upon them. This knowledge engenders not pride but thanksgiving and praise and sincere and keen-sighted humility.

But are there no dangers attached to this habit of self-scrutiny? There are; and none knew this better than the saints. They had practical experience of these possible evil effects, and they inveighed against them in language which has been wrongfully applied to the habit of reflection in itself. St Jane de Chantal experienced something very similar to what St Theresa felt when she described so graphically the danger she felt in herself, but which she conquered, of yielding to sadness, melancholy, and nervous depression. "I dare not read that letter over again," she writes, "for fear of reopening the door to reflections and thoughts about what is passing in my soul, owing to the overactivity of my mind." This remark must not be isolated from its context. The "activity" she dreads is an activity which becomes a weakness by reacting on itself, and which by contemplating itself destroys simplicity and diminishes energy. "Avoid *useless* reflections," she writes elsewhere. Next to useless reflections come those which are dangerous, because they arise from self-complacency, self-love, and sometimes from a kind of laziness which prefers to contemplate and analyse itself rather than take the trouble to conquer its hesitations and langour. "Everything in its proper season," is a lesson the great foundress is not inclined to let us forget. "In times of suffering, suffer; in times of action, act; in times of joy, rejoice humbly without fear of doing harm thereby to anything. Such a thought can only arise from self-love." No less dangerous than self-love, which deceives the heart, is the imagination, which leads the understanding and judgment astray. To pay it attention is to encourage it, and, therefore, the saint writes to one of her nuns: " I believe that what you experience comes from God; still, do not pay too much attention to it for fear of self-complacency. Do not examine too closely whether or not your imagination may have a share in it; one look is sufficient to bring it into play." The saint is a good psychologist! And what deep knowledge of the human heart is contained in the following passage: "You tell me three things which augur badly of our novice's frame of mind: that she is attached to her own will and opinion, that she has no simplicity, and that she is immersed in self-contemplation. . If she has a good head it will only make her the more dangerous; for great minds, when not addicted to solid and mortified piety, bring desolation upon a whole monastery and sometimes upon a whole order." [1]

If we now read over again the two articles of Issy, we shall see that they are a very accurate *resumé* of the united experiences of the saints, set forth with all their known ability for putting things in their right time and place, without exaggeration or omission.

The same principle may be applied to the so-called

[1] See Letters, edition already quoted, pp. 282, 420, 448, 476, etc.

"passive" state of prayer, the prayer of quiet or union. We must not forget that, even in the case of great saints, this state is never more than temporary, nor does it occur until late on in the life of sanctity. It is, as it were, the repose in the working day of a good labourer. It comes as the reward of prolonged effort, the slowly acquired results of which it, as it were, crowns; but it is not an end in itself, it stimulates to further efforts which it makes more easy and more fruitful. St John of the Cross tells us that for a long time " images, ideas, knowledge, reasoning, mental prayer, material objects which strike the senses and imagination, are necessary to prepare the soul for the interior life and perfection." Only quite at the end does it become expedient to rise above the kind of mental activity which is natural to us. Between these two kinds of operation there exists the same sort of difference as there is between a thing that is in process of doing and a thing which is already accomplished—between what we desire to acquire and what we actually possess. " Excepting at such times as these the soul should make use, in her spiritual exercises, in all her actions and works, of the memory and of meditation, in order to increase both her devotion and the good she gains from them. She must, above all, meditate upon the life, passion, and death of our Saviour, in order that her actions and life may become conformable to His."[1]

It is therefore as great a mistake to believe that the saint necessarily and habitually suspends the

---

[1] Edition already quoted, p. 145.

operations of his mind, as it is to think that great men are somnambulists who unknowingly receive suggestions and inspirations from the Unconscious. People have readily enough accepted the theory that inspiration in great men is accumulated thought which gives itself out in flashes like the lightning from clouds overcharged with electricity. May not the so-called passive contemplation of great mystics be likewise accumulated piety, active meditation, and resolve?

Bossuet tells us that not only do "spoken words," which are the term of discursive operations and efforts, necessarily precede this state of prayer, but that even while it lasts, the state of passivity is by no means universal or continuous. "The soul gives itself as the spouse to her lover. It gives itself to God as actively and freely as God gives Himself to it, for God raises its power of free election to its highest pitch on account of the desire He has to be chosen freely. This is what St Clement of Alexandria means when he says that man predestines God as much as God predestines man."[1]

Such then are "those operations which are higher" than discursive operations. St Theresa treats of them beautifully[2] when she speaks of souls who, without losing (far from it) their recollection and knowledge of mysteries, become capable of seizing them "by a single look" and only appear unable to speak about them, because they enjoy in complete repose, everything that has been engraved upon

[1] Bossuet, "On States of Prayer." Treatise I., Book VII.
[2] See in particular "The Interior Castle," p. 499.

their memory and made present to their minds by previous meditations. But while they thus gather into one single action the operations which have gone before, they are not rendered incapable of further reflections. Bossuet, at least, did not think so when he wrote: "It would seem that the extreme simplicity of this kind of prayer renders it less easy of recognition in itself than in its effects."

Neither did St Theresa look upon it as the inmost chamber in her Interior Castle, for the characteristic feature of the progress she made during the last five years of her life, was the possession and the exercise, calm indeed, but more vigorous than ever, of that "Apostolic strength," which she derived from her raptures and visions.

CHAPTER V

FEELING, LOVE AND ACTION

IT is an easier task to dispel prejudice by showing that the saints are people who love very intensely and whose love is, as it were, their very life. Before attempting to do so, however, I wish to say a few words on the subject of the "sensibility" of the saints.

Christian philosophy teaches that feeling, or what St Thomas, who uses the word in a very general sense, calls simply passion, belongs not to the soul alone but to body and soul together (*Passio per se convenit composito*[1]); or, in other words, that the complex phenomena of joy and pain, passion and emotion, are determined by the joint influence of physical and mental states. To my mind, it is impossible to deny that a man's feelings are coloured to a great extent by his habits of mind, good or bad education, trained or untrained reasoning faculties, by the natural bent of his imagination, his ideas, and above all by his religious beliefs. At the same time, it is equally certain that these emotions are keen or languid, intense or calm, according to the sensations we experience of

---

[1] Some modern thinkers, in their attempts to combat purely intellectualist theories, have returned to this tradition, adding to it many certainly very interesting facts and some scarcely tenable assumptions. See the *Correspondant* of April 25th, 1897.

physical disturbances, of correlated and sympathetic movements, and of those many reflex operations caused by the modifications of one organ affecting all the others.

The emotional sensibility of the saints is subject to these ordinary laws, and is therefore determined, in the first instance, by natural temperament. As women are usually more sensitive and emotional than men, we must not be surprised to find that this rule holds good of women saints no less than of ordinary women. According to Schopenhauer, "women pay their debt to life, not by action, but by suffering,"[1] and if this dictum is correct, it must be especially applicable to the heroines of the Church. It is so obvious that physical constitution must largely account for this fact that I do not see any necessity of going to work to prove it. What is of more interest to determine is whether the key to all manifestations of sensibility in the saints is to be found in the modifications to which their physical existence was subjected.

Some people think — and their opinion has been apparently confirmed by Claude Bernard — that sensibility is a faculty which is influenced solely by the heart and brain and that the feelings are absolutely independent of all the other organs of the body. No one denies that the heart and brain are the organs which have principally to do with the feelings. A thought may involuntarily present itself to the mind and be rejected, or it may be voluntarily

---

[1] "And by love," adds M. Fouilleé, and in my opinion he is right.

admitted, retained and dwelt on, but in either case the movements of the heart are affected and that organ is subjected to a pressure, more or less great. —The result is that the blood is either given out violently from the heart, causing a suffusion of blood to the brain when the face becomes crimson; or else the blood is held back in the heart, circulation is impeded, the face becomes pallid, and the subject generally goes off into a dead faint.

This is true certainly, but it is not the whole truth. There are many other organs which help to modify both our feelings and our sensations, for on the one hand, whether by their healthy action or by their secretions, they affect those nerves upon which the harmonious action of the larger organs depends, and on the other, they themselves suffer indirectly from the movements of the heart when they are either left without blood or receive it in too large quantities. This was long ago noticed by an observer whose opinion is certainly worthy of attention:[1] " The experimental science of our days compels us to determine more accurately the various elements of this phenomenon, but by no means allows us to deny its existence. Perhaps it even exaggerates its importance when, on the strength of certain pathological facts and experiments of the dissecting room, it affirms that a more or less artificial anæsthesia of the skin and the mucous membrane and other parts can induce an apparent suspension of every sort of emotional activity."

[1] See Dr Sollier's article in the *Revue philosophique* of March 1894.

Anyway our forefathers were right when they attached so great an importance to the action of the heart and gave a lesser share in the work to the other organs. They were keen observers, though they may have expressed themselves badly.

Were they right too when they declared the heart to be the organ of the nobler feelings, of courage, love, enthusiasm, of moral suffering generously accepted, and when they attributed feelings of secret envy and jealousy and gnawing melancholy to the influence of other organs? Apparently they were, and a very possible explanation of the fact lies in the most intimate connection existing between the heart and the brain, which is the organ of those higher impressions that are more directly controlled and determined by the action of our free will.

Human life, we must not forget, is a complexus of actions and reactions in which body and soul alternately modify one another. If it comprises innate peculiarities of structure or tendency which dispose us to one passion more than another, it also comprises self-formed voluntary habits which check or accelerate this disposition, and create more or less powerful currents amongst these mixed emotions.

Hagiographers constantly tell us, apropos of their subjects, that anger, hatred and pain cause the blood-vessels to contract, retard the action of the humours, and produce obstructions; while hope, joy and Divine love "which is ever well regulated," expand the heart and the blood-vessels, "quicken the circulation and raise the spirits." This was the old way of speaking, and it is more in harmony with modern physiological theories than people generally suppose.[1]

To go back now to our saints. If we remember the kind of life led by the majority of them, we see at once that their temperance, continency and austerity must have had the effect of greatly simplifying the movements of the physical and animal parts of their organisation.

Over the door of each cell at the Grande Chartreuse there is a Latin inscription. The first one that I saw when I visited the place bore the words "*Estote sobrii, simplices et quieti,*" a beautiful graduation of ideas, in which the first leads on, of necessity, to the two others. The composer was evidently of one mind with the greatest moralist of antiquity, for twice over Seneca tells us that "luxury feeds anger," and again, "what chiefly feeds anger is luxury and self-indulgence."[2] Though seemingly paradoxical, these words express a great truth and one which I have often seen verified among the criminal classes, where, in spite of the prejudices entertained on the subject by worldly-minded persons, the chief offenders are not those who suffer but those who live in comfort. But we must not stray from our subject. All I want to point out is that owing to physiological reaction no less than to the combined

---

[1] See Appendix.
[2] Luxury is a relative term. What would seem homely enough to a Parisian would excite pride and sensuality in a simple villager.

effects of habits to which all the faculties, and even the mind, are subject, the allaying of the appetites is necessarily followed by the allaying of a considerable amount of sensibility.

This rule does not apply in the case of the heart, properly so-called, and of that kind of emotion which is controlled by it. The account of the *post-mortem* examination[1] on the body of St Philip Neri is a most interesting document. In this case, the inferior organs were atrophied, but the heart had increased in size to such an extent that, in order to make room for itself, it had forced up one of the ribs and created a sort of artificial cavity. This would account for the rapidity of his circulation and the great heat of his body, which no extreme of cold could affect, and we may be allowed to conjecture that it would also account for those outbursts of racy humour which were intermingled with his effusions of ardent love, as, for instance, when he declared that "there is nothing harder than living to the man who really loves God."

It is a well-known fact that singular phenomena in the physiological organ of the heart are very frequent among the saints. I am not going to discuss the more extraordinary of these cases, or those which Catholic sentiment treats as genuinely miraculous, like the piercing of St Theresa's heart or those visions in which some mystics have felt as if Christ gave them His Heart in exchange for theirs.

---

[1] Performed by Cesalpino and two other celebrated surgeons of the day. A similar account is given of the results of the *post-mortem* examination on the remains of Père de Condren.

It is open to anyone, of course, to believe that these are mostly tricks of the imagination, which from a corporal sensation conjures up a symbolical vision and innocently believes it to be a reality. Still, the person has experienced some physical change in this part of the body, for, even were the miracle genuine, it would call natural forces into play, and the results of these material changes, whether in the heart itself, or in organs which shew signs of an afflux of blood or stigmata, have been frequently verified by authentic official reports.

B. Angela of Foligno gives the following account of herself: "When I saw Jesus Christ clearly, with the eyes of my soul, poor, despised and suffering as I had asked to see Him, I felt such a piercing sorrow that I thought my heart would break."

Many sensitive people could say almost as much of the effect produced upon them by any great trial that has to come to them during their lives. St Mary Magdalen of Pazzi had a more wonderful experience. Our Lord appeared to her one day and shewed her His Heart, and she was ever after "obliged to unfasten her habit, or to burst forth into torrents of words like songs, in order to lessen the heat of the interior fire which consumed her."

St Catherine of Genoa believed that she had a wound in her breast, and she was often obliged to keep her hand on her heart to quiet its palpitations. Eighteen months after her death, her body was exhumed and found to be incorrupt. The skin had turned yellow, "with the exception of the skin over the heart, which was still quite red." Similar, and even more wonderful phenomena were observed in the case of the hearts of St Francis of Sales and St Jane de Chantal.

There is no need for me to supplement the very able and authentic accounts that have been published of these marvellous occurrences. All I wish to say is, that they shew that the sensibility of the saints was of that warm, human kind which points to a close connection between body and soul, between the circulation of the blood and the movements of the mind.

We see therefore, that in judging of the sensibility of the saints, we must take account, less of their capacity for joy or suffering, than of their will to suffer in the interests of some one cause or idea. Faith controls love and love controls those mental images which excite the emotions and thereby reveal the interior feelings of the heart. The world readily believes that the mystic has lost all power of feeling, because he is no longer moved by the things of this earth, but the mystic himself considers that his feelings were, so to say, dead during the years which preceded his conversion, and that they have been recalled to life by the action of grace. "My heart was then so hard," says St Theresa, "that I could read the whole Passion without shedding a single tear. This want of feeling greatly distressed me." She tells us again that "these tears, which are, in a way, the result of our own persevering efforts, helped by grace, are of immense value, and it would be worth all the labours in the world, to obtain even a single one of them."

Does the saint who thus suffers with Christ, cease to feel his own pains? Does he no longer feel the movements of the passions like other men? This is sometimes the case, but, according to Benedict XIV., it more frequently happens that the senses are only under control and not extinguished. The following words of St Bernard[1] can be used both of physical martyrdom with its attendant material tortures and of that moral martyrdom which is endured by great souls. "Where, then, is the soul of the martyr? It is in a place of safety, dwelling in the Bosom of Jesus. If it were dwelling in its own, by self-scrutiny, assuredly the stabbing sword would be seen and felt, the pain would be unendurable, it would succumb or deny its Lord. If it is an exile from the body, is it wonderful that it does not feel the pains of the body? This is not the consequence of insensibility but of the force of love." *Non stupor sed amor*,—a definition at once classical and strictly scientific, and one which will help us clearly to distinguish between the psychological condition of the saints and that of all those persons whose state bears an artificial resemblance to theirs — buddhist monks, fakirs, invalids, and since we must mention them once more, hysterical subjects.

M. Janet has called St Theresa " the patroness " of hysterical persons, but did the thought of her

[1] Sermon 61 (quoted by many of the saints, who probably recognised in these words their own experiences).

and those like her, never recur to his mind when treating of emotional perturbations? For though, like his predecessors, he lays great stress upon the fact that hysterical attacks are the means by which "exaggerated and perverted" emotions manifest themselves, he is careful to point out that the dominant idea in the mind of the hysterical subject, develops in an unbalanced and disconnected manner. From this latter remark he is led to another which is in only apparent contradiction with it. Hysterical subjects, he says, have really far fewer emotions than is generally believed, " for their chief characteristic, in this respect as in others, is a diminution in the number of psychological phenomena. Persons suffering from hysteria are usually indifferent to everything that does not bear reference to a small number of fixed ideas. Although their emotions are exaggerated and out of all proportion, they are few and monotonous."

I am pretty sure that if St Theresa, who has given us such an astonishingly accurate description of the four kinds of melancholy, were to read these lines, she would recognise the condition they describe as that of more than one of the nuns she was obliged to nurse.[1]

But who could possibly apply the above description to natures so many-sided and richly endowed as those

---

[1] Especially of the poor ecstatica whom she cured by making her take more food. Compare M. Janet's recipe with St Theresa's. He says, " With rest, better food and more sleep, the sick person often improves, and then she regains the feelings which had disappeared."

of St Theresa, St Jane de Chantal, St Bernard, and St Francis of Sales.

Someone may answer: "All the same, great saints were absolutely disabled by their emotions at the sight of a crucifix, while they could hear that a revolution had broken out and not turn a hair." It may be so, but then many persons who make this an objection against the saints, are themselves ready to weep over a novel, while they remain quite unmoved by the story of the Passion of Christ, which He endured to save mankind.

However, the most subtle part of the accusation levelled against the saints is really contained in these words: "Hysterical subjects lose those social and altruistic feelings which are the most complex of all."[1]

Do the saints lose these feelings?

In order to answer this question we must not only continue our study of their outward characteristics, but we must probe even still more deeply into the hidden psychology of their lives. To begin with, whom do the saints love? The answer, of course, will be,—God. Nobody doubts that fact for a single instant, and the tendency is, on the contrary, to exaggerate it, and to say that the saints love nobody but God.

We must not forget that in sanctity, as in all things else, there is a gradual development. (Plato would

[1] They ought to be, but the question is whether they really are. It is terribly easy for a cynic like La Rochefoucauld to simplify this complexity by attributing all our social inclinations to self-love. If this ruthless moralist is right, I leave it to my readers to decide which head the cap is most likely to fit: the average individual's or the saint's.

call it a "dialectic"[1] and in the present day it would be called an evolution.) It is a mistake to think that the high-water mark of sanctity is reached on the day the saint makes the sacrifices which are most painful to nature. The monk, the religious, lives on long after he has severed the last ties that bind him to the world. It was not the only time that St Jane de Chantal acted as a saint when she stepped across the prostrate body of her son. On the contrary, her subsequent life of sanctity was the only possible justification for such an action. St John of the Cross has already told us that we must pass through a certain night of the senses and memory in order to enjoy that full light of the imagination and mind which illuminates even the things of earth. The saint has also to pass through a night of the heart, but he does not remain in it. On the day after her clothing, a nun[2] wrote as follows: " In obedience to the rule of the noviciate, I have dropped all my correspondence. Sacrifices of the heart and universal detachment are what God chiefly requires of us, poor women, who have nothing left on this earth, neither country, home, parents or friends." Having got that far, she pulls herself up and continues, without even beginning a fresh sentence: —"or rather, I ought to say, the whole world is ours, for, according to St Vincent of Paul, our love embraces the entire world."

[1] *i.e.*, a logical, as opposed to a physical unfolding; the articulated expansion of an idea rather than of an organism.—[Ed.].
[2] See Life of *Mother Marie de Sales-Chappuis* (of the Visitation in the Rue de Vaugirard), p. 353.

This young religious was speaking in the language of the saints. Before St Vincent of Paul, St Catherine of Siena used to say: "The reason why God's servants love creatures so much is that they see how much Christ loves them, and it is one of the properties of love to love what is loved by the persons we love." She constantly repeats the same idea.[1] We are told by her contemporaries that she brought about innumerable reconciliations, and that this was the chief cause of the great influence she exercised over the public affairs of her country. Many other saints whose lives and actions were more hidden than hers, have said the same thing, that when Christ crucified takes possession of a soul He inspires it with a very great tenderness for the humanity for which He died. Sanctity demands complete detachment from all pleasures which are derived from self-love. This is a rule which admits of no exception, and it applies to spiritual as well as earthly consolations. According to the great mystics, the end and chief use of "dryness and aridities" is to detach the soul, not from spiritual benefits, but from a selfish and sensible love of them. Once self-love is destroyed, the barrier is done away with and not only is there no law of detachment from all things, but the soul is enjoined to love everything, provided that it does so "for the love of God."

I foresee an objection. I shall be told that loving the whole world really means loving no one and that this universal love is precisely what kills the natural affections. But is it loving no one to do as the saints

[1] See "Letters," I. 237, II. 327.

did when they deprived themselves of food and clothing for the sake of the poor, when they nursed the sick and even kissed their wounds, when they entertained pilgrims and strangers gratuitously, when they found homes for orphans and children, and braved the contagion of lepers and the plague-stricken with no other protection than faith and prayer, when they freed captives at the price of their own liberty, and enfranchised slaves, when they defended negroes against the tyranny of their masters and, like St Catherine of Siena, assisted convicts at the hour of death, when they founded refuges for young girls whose poverty exposed them to evil, and opened their arms to the afflicted and to sinners for whom they felt all Christ's passionate pity and mercy? There is no priest, no apostle, no father worthy of the name, who ought not to be able to cry out at every hour of the day with St Paul—"Who is weak and I am not weak, who is scandalised and I am not on fire?" Who suffers in any way and I do not suffer with him?

Natural affection is, I think, equally strong in all the saints, though their manner of shewing it varies according to the condition of life in which they are placed. Married saints are model husbands and wives in the intensity of their human affection. St Bridget, St Lewis, St Elizabeth of Hungary and St Jane de Chantal found their earthly love no hindrance to divine love—very possibly the former led them on to the latter, for every duty of our state of life which we fulfil with all our heart, leads us nearer to God. If the love of an earthly father teaches the child to understand the love of its Father in Heaven, why should not a woman's affection for her earthly husband lead her on to a more tender love of Him who in mystical language is so often called the Spouse of the Soul? St Bernard[1] went so far as to say, "Love begins in the flesh and ends in the spirit," and St Catherine of Siena tells us emphatically that nothing has so great an influence over the heart of man as love, "for man was created by love and therefore it is his nature to love. Man was created body and soul by love, for out of love God created him to His own image and likeness and out of love his parents gave him being."

When from the contemplation of her Heavenly Spouse, the soul returns to earth and to her earthly spouse, she returns with a love that is purified certainly, but in no way diminished. The saints apparently found it easy to reconcile these two kinds of love, for in their daily lives they passed rapidly and without long preparation from one to the other. St Elizabeth of Hungary exerted all her ingenuity in order to leave her husband as little as she could, for, says a contemporary writer, they loved one another above what it is possible to conceive (*supra quam credi valeat*). When she found out accidentally, one day, that her husband had promised to join the Crusade, her grief was so violent that she fainted away. When left alone, she returned to her penitential exercises as eagerly as if she had had no love for anyone but God, but when her husband

[1] Ep. II. Quoted in the new "Life of St Bernard" by Abbé Vacandard, I. 183.

returned she dressed herself according to her rank and as magnificently as possible in order to please him, although her natural beauty and their great mutual love made this, strictly speaking, unnecessary. The simple, homely old Latin chronicles describe how she mortified herself severely in the evening before going sweetly and gaily to share her husband's bed,[1] (*ad lectumque mariti reversa hilarem se exhibuit et jucundam*). And when from prayer with God, she returned to her duties as a woman, her love went out not only to her husband, but to the poor, to beggars, debtors, to the sick and dying. She even wrapt the dead in sheets taken from her own bed and followed the poorest of her subjects to the grave.

Some people will say: this is all very well, but how about the saints who left their families and the world? I answer that they broke their dearest ties only in order to renew them in a different manner, and that this renewing was voluntary on their part and in obedience to a want of their very nature. Most of those who have left father and mother could re-echo these words of St Theresa: " I am only telling the truth, for I remember it distinctly, that when I left my father's house, I felt pain like that which one feels in one's agony and I do not believe that death itself can be more painful. I felt as if all my bones were being torn apart."[2]

The soul of the saint, therefore, returns to the

---

[1] I need not refer my readers to Montalembert's delightful "Life of St Elizabeth." Paris: Lecoffre.

[2] Her life, p. 30.

things of earth with its human affections undiminished, and also with a new love that it has acquired by contact with the Heart of Christ. It is free to exercise both the one and the other in its relations with those who are bound to it by the ties of duty, nature and friendship.

St Jane Chantal was not an exception to all rule, when, after having founded her Order, she set to work to marry her daughters and start her son in life. She won from the latter the singular testimony that if she had remained in the world her maternal love and "unexampled prudence" could not have done more for him than she accomplished from her convent.[1] She does not stand alone in her intense love for her family and in the grief, going so far as to endanger her life, which she felt at losing them, and in her sympathy when they themselves lost husband or child.

The great Carmelite saint followed the fortunes of her brothers and sisters from the seclusion of her cell, established them in life, found them partners, took interest in their lives and gave them good advice. If faith does not loosen family ties with the ordinary believer, who knows that they will be continued in the next world, how could it do so with a saint like St Theresa, who lets us into the secrets of her heart when she tells us: "I was carried up to Heaven, and the first persons I saw there were my father and mother."

Souls like hers are convinced that not only can "no one have too much intelligence" but also that

[1] See Mgr. Bougaud's "Life of St Chantal," II. 39, cf. ib., 417.

"no one can have too much heart, and that if only the intention is pure we should love every creature on this earth." The former assertion I find re-echoed by St Catherine of Siena, St Theresa, and also by the stern founder of St Sulpice, M. Olier. Writing to condole with the Marquis de Fénelon on the death of his wife, he says:[1] "My dear child, your Madeleine is loving you and waiting for you in the Bosom of God. She knows that you cannot love her too much." I venture therefore to affirm that when two souls are united "in God" they cannot love each other too much. This was M. Olier's opinion and that of the saints also.

As regards the second assertion, that we should love every creature on this earth, it is justified by the simple affection shewn by the saints for animals. Everyone is delighted, and rightly, by St Francis of Assisi's expressions of tenderness for his little sisters, the doves. The only mistake is, that people fancy these are peculiar to himself, the effect of his gentle, dreamy, innocent nature, which was far more affectionate and poetical than is usual with the saints.

St Bernard, though fiery and awe-inspiring by nature, and very severe to himself, was seized with feelings of intense compassion at the sight of pain, weakness and moral or physical infirmity. He could not attend a stranger's funeral without shedding tears. His kindness of heart shewed itself, say his biographers, even towards animals and wild beasts. If he saw a hare pursued by dogs, or a small bird in danger of being caught by a bird of prey, he was so

[1] Letters, I. 515.

touched with compassion that he could not help making the sign of the cross in the air to ensure the poor little creature's safety.[1] We see, therefore, that that emotional sensibility which the saints at first endeavour to diminish by refusing it the satisfaction it craves for, returns to them later on, having gained in richness and delicacy from the intensity of their love and the unlimited area embraced by their charity.

This same sensibility makes them not indifferent to those innocent pleasures which, according to Alfred de Musset, help us to enjoy life, or at any rate, make the burden of it easier to bear. They do not seek them for themselves, but they endeavour to procure them for others, especially for the young, or the sick and afflicted. St Clare and St Theresa used to drag themselves out of their beds in order to go and see if any of their sisters, whose health caused them anxiety, were warmly clothed enough. St Francis of Assisi almost worked a miracle in order to procure " a good dinner " for his doctor, one day that the monastery larder was nearly empty. On the other hand, however austere to himself the saint may be, he readily accepts a service from another, when it is offered, merely thanking God for having given him so kind a companion.

The friendships of the saints are therefore no matter for astonishment, although a certain well-known writer has expressed a wish to write a whole book on the subject. Neither is it surprising that " in the history of most of those saints who have

---

[1] See Vacandard — work quoted above, II. 514; also see Appendix.

reformed or founded religious institutions, we find that the love and devotedness of a holy woman exercised a great influence over their lives and work." St Paula stands beside St Jerome, the Countess Matilda beside St Gregory VII., St Clare beside St Francis of Assisi, St Theresa beside St John of the Cross, St Jane de Chantal beside St Francis of Sales.

It is now time to turn to the consideration of that love which transforms all other love—the love of God.

I shall consider it under two aspects only—in its relation to suffering and in its relation to action, for it is under these two aspects that the love of the saints differs absolutely, not only from profane love, which seeks its own enjoyment, but also from the " quietist " love of false mystics.

" I have always recognised," writes M. Olier to a holy woman—his confidant at the time being—called Marie Rousseau, " that to suffer is the very essence of being a Christian."[1] And yet he goes on to tell her of his many troubles and of his dread of the trials of life. He bore them, nevertheless, with heroic courage, and in another letter, written shortly afterwards to his director, he explains why he was able to do so. " How easy it is," he says, " to love in the midst of enjoyment. But to love in the midst of suffering is hard, and in my opinion this is the test of true love."

There are two ways of loving in the midst of suffering. A person may accept sufferings with

[1] Letters, I. 276, *cf. ib.*, 390.

resignation for the sake of obtaining future happiness for himself or others. This is the first degree to which the saints soon attained, and none sooner than the writer whose words we have been quoting. But from this acceptance of suffering which is within the reach of many philosophers and men of heroic character, he rose to a desire of suffering. Why did he desire to suffer?

There are degrees even of this latter state. Suffering may be desired, not as the reward of a kind of self-interested devotion, but as a condition in which we are brought nearer to the attainment of an object which is, in itself, worth all the sacrifices of which man is capable. "Become like to the meek Jesus your Chief," writes St Catherine of Siena to Urban VI., "whose will it is, that from the beginning of the world until the end, nothing great shall ever be accomplished without much suffering." [1]

In spite of the heroism of her words, it is likely enough that the saint was making some allowance for a remains of human feeling in the Sovereign Pontiff, and that she strove to turn his love of glory to good account. But when the saint rises to fresh heights he realises that all great things are in reality accomplished by God through the medium of man, and therefore as far as he himself is concerned he desires suffering solely as a means of destroying self-love and everything that tends to separate him from the Object of his love. We read in M. Olier's life:

[1] Letters, I. 83.

FEELING, LOVE AND ACTION

"I said interiorly: Lord, by suffering alone, can I shew my love for Thee. Lord, how can I live without expressing my love for Thee. Suffering for Thy sake will shew Thee that I love Thee."

There is a human element even in heroism such as this.[1] A brave soldier desires to fight for his country's glory, and a statesman who is passionately desirous of his country's greatness will grudge the time wasted in the pleasures of society.—Did not Lord Palmerston declare ironically, but also with a great deal of truth, that "Life would be endurable were it not for its pleasures." Why should the saints alone be considered mad when, full of zeal for the kingdom of God, they cry out with St Theresa: "Suffering alone can make life tolerable to me. My greatest desire is to suffer. Often and often I cry out to God from the depths of my soul: Lord, either to suffer or to die is all I ask of Thee."[2]

And when the saint has thus accepted and desired sufferings, he is not satisfied unless he courts them. This is asceticism properly so-called. People get a false idea on the subject and imagine that in the

---

[1] I found the following remarkable lines in a dramatic leaflet of Jules Lemâitre, *Débats*, Aug. 11, 1895:—"Oh! the wonderful fertility of pain. It is suffering which makes Jocelyn's heart so deep, so wide, so tender—with great souls their capacity for loving brings suffering, which is the sign and the measure of this capacity, and then suffering, in its turn, increases and ennobles the power of loving—so that very soon such souls can only be filled and satisfied by taking upon themselves, by charity, all the sufferings of others."

[2] Her life, 351. *Cf.* Olier, Letters, I. 390.

saints, asceticism comes from a distaste for life or from a desire to mortify gross temptations of the flesh. But asceticism, if we look out the etymology of the word, means exercise. And in what way does the ascetic exercise himself? In bearing sufferings patiently, then in seeking them in spite of his natural dislike of them, and finally, in acquiring a love for them. Quite so, and this is the gradual advance we described above. But when he suffers voluntarily, the saint exercises himself in yet another way. He exercises himself in willing and acting, and this brings us back to the consideration that according to the theoretical psychology of the saints, love and the will are one and the same thing.

A superficial psychology, or one which deals only with persons very far removed in character from the saints, would have us believe that pleasure stimulates action and that pain dulls it. Pain dulls action when it saps the strength, when it is dreaded and the person either cannot or will not turn it to good account, or when effort would only end in creating irreparable evil. But this is never the case with the saints. With them sufferings may reduce the strength of the body, but they do not weaken the soul, for they are the fruit of the vigour of a soul which loves and is desirous only of self-sacrifice. Neither do sufferings dull action, for though they are increased by it, this increase is precisely what the soul most desires, as the highest degree of perfection to which it can attain on this earth. Finally, they do no injury to the soul, for they are the most efficacious means by which nature can be repaired and restored to its ideal state. This state is attained in its perfection only in the next world, but the soul is cheered and encouraged by possessing a foretaste of it here below. This foretaste produces in the soul of the saint a certain joy[1] which never leaves it, and this joy co-exists with sufferings which are not only not dreaded but which are sought after and encouraged.

Two apparently incompatible states are in this way brought together in a union which is incomprehensible to those who only know commonplace humanity in its dull mediocrity of useless existence but which is perfectly intelligible and susceptible of being scientifically explained to those who look at psychology as a whole which takes in all the parts of the human soul in their right order and excellence.

Action is therefore the culminating point in the life of sanctity, but instead of having now arrived at the term, we stand rather on the threshold of a complete study of the saint's career; for however sublime his words or sentiments may be, it is by his actions that men judge him and by his actions that even sceptics are brought to honour and admire him.[2]

As my limits are already reached, I will only make a short summary of what I have been saying, and conclude by shewing how, in the saints, aptitude for action and the power of acting are closely con-

---

[1] This joy has been proved to be so inseparably allied with the state of sanctity that Benedict XIV. makes its presence one of the necessary conditions for beatification.

[2] This volume is to be followed by lives of the saints which purpose to shew sanctity in action.

nected with those psychological phenomena we have been considering above.

"He does much who loves much," says the author of the "Imitation," and it is certainly true that love itself—that is to say, love considered as an impulse of the soul which feels itself at once too rich and too poor, and which seeks to give itself and thereby to realise itself—is active and well worthy of the following description: "Love feeleth no burden, thinketh nothing of labours, would willingly do more than it can, complaineth not of impossibility because it conceiveth that it may and can do all things" (Im., Bk. III. chap. 5).

But we must not forget that "it is the property of love to change the soul into the thing which it loves,"[1] and therefore those who have charge of a soul are in fear of its safety until they have seen what the object of its love is to be. As the soul of the saint loves God and the Son of God, it is not deterred from action, but on the contrary it is constrained to follow Him, carrying its own cross. Like St Catherine of Siena,[2] it considers that its neighbour has been given to it as a means of proving its love for God. As it cannot serve God directly, it serves Him indirectly to the best of its ability, according to its state of life, in the person of its neighbour who is dear to God.

If, in the accomplishment of its task, the soul meets with sensible consolations, it receives them with gratitude, but if they are denied to it, it remembers that true love is shewn by gratuitous

---

[1] Olier, Letters, II. 423.   [2] Letters, II. 285.

labour and not by feelings of sensible devotion. St John of the Cross and St Theresa both declare that love is before all things strong and efficacious, and that to love God means to serve Him in humility, strength and justice.

Action is necessary to the saints on account of their desire for suffering and also on account of the kind of suffering they desire. They have no love of passive suffering or sadness, and they cannot find words enough in which to condemn it. St Francis of Assisi calls it the "Babylonian" malady, and St Catherine of Siena says that it is brought on by Satan, who, when he sees that he cannot tempt the soul to sensuality, which "destroys constancy, and renders the heart narrow, weak and cowardly," endeavours to excite "trouble, disgust, sadness and scruples of conscience." M. Olier also says that sadness inclines the soul to desire sensible consolations which, although they appear to come from God, are in reality born of sensuality and self-deception. St Theresa tells us plainly, "I fear nothing so much as to see my daughters lose this joy of the soul, for I know, to my cost, what a discontented religious is like."

The saints, therefore, love active sufferings, or to use their own words, the pangs of travail. For a single soul, for a city or a country, for an institution which hatred would endeavour to suppress, for an Order which is to be laborious, learned and charitable, for a church, they rejoice to feel those pangs of spiritual child-birth, and in the language of all true mystics, such child-bearing is the fruit and token of love.

I am not asserting a paradox when I say that the activity of the saints is nourished by contemplation, although Rénan has contrasted saints and men of action with the intention of showing that the former were idealists and men of prayer and contemplation only. His mistake is shared by a good many people, but it is none the less amazing on that account.[1]

There is, as we have seen, one faculty which remains not only unfettered but strong and active, while the saint is wrapt in the highest kind of contemplation, and that is the intellectual will. The senses, memory, imagination, reasoning powers, and the effective will may be for a time paralysed, but the simple action of the will which consists in the free gift of one's self, is never suspended. All true mystics agree as to this point. And again, psychological facts must be judged of by their development and effects. Contemplation is, we have seen, closely connected with love, and what is more, with active love. It is the fruit of an already intense and active love, and it inspires and directs a love that is still more ardent. In the midst of a life of action, St Gregory the Great writes: " If we wish to reach the citadel of contemplation, we must begin by exercising ourselves in the field of labour. Whoever wishes to give himself to contemplation, must first examine what

---

[1] It is not shared by Henri Martin, who writes as follows of Joan of Arc: "She was a serious child, already shewing signs of that love of solitude and meditation combined with great energy of action, which is characteristic of persons called to fulfil a great mission in life."

degree of love he is capable of; for love is the lever of the soul. It alone is able to raise the soul, to detach it from this world and give it wings."[1] Here work is made to precede contemplation and contemplation, in its turn, produces work and makes it more efficacious. It is impossible for the purified soul to contemplate the Passion of Christ without feeling called to suffer with Him, in the same spirit and with the same end in view—the redemption of mankind.

Contemplation is also a help to action, because it forms, in the soul, as it were, a reservoir of ideas, love, and energy, which when full is forced to overflow. "A duct-pipe," says St Bernard, "gives out at once whatever it receives, a reservoir waits until it is full." He goes on to add: "Unfortunately there are in the Church very few reservoirs and many duct-pipes,—souls who desire to rule without having learned to govern themselves."

Lastly, the active strength of the saints is due to their state of mind and to their firm and enlightened faith. They are, as I said before, certain of their end, but prudent and circumspect in the means they use to gain it. Here again, the saint and the sceptic act very differently. The sceptic adopts any means that come to hand, but he is quickly discouraged, for he very soon begins to ask himself, "What is the good of it?" The saint neither doubts nor hesitates, once he has begun to act, precisely because, before acting, he has hesitated, doubted and reflected. "When the soul acts purely

[1] Moralia, vi. 37.

for the love of God," says St Theresa, " He allows it to experience, I know not what sort of fear, when it first begins to act." But she would have agreed with St M. Magdalen of Pazzi, who says that the servant of God " at the plough, never turns his head to look back," and with the advice given us by St Ignatius: " In times of desolation never to change the resolutions made before the desolation began, but to try and change the interior dispositions, that is to say, the desolation itself."

Let us stop for a moment to consider this rule, which is one of the wisest ever drawn up by a director of souls.

What are these two states of consolation and desolation? There can be no better definition given of them than we find in the Exercises of St Ignatius. He sums up the teaching of tradition as the subjects in the following words: " I call consolation, every increase of faith, hope and charity and every kind of interior joy which calls and attracts man to heavenly things and to the salvation of his own soul, rendering it quiet and tranquil in its Creator and Lord. . I call desolation all that is contrary. . as darkness and disquiet of soul, an attraction towards low and earthly things, the disquiet of various agitations and temptations which urge it to diffidence, when the soul finds itself without hope and without love, slothful, tepid, and sad, and, as it were, separated from its Creator and Lord."

So that what is called by the saints " the good spirit," is that which causes joy even in the midst of sufferings that are both accepted and desired, and "the bad spirit" is that which causes doubt and sadness even in the midst of sensible pleasures. This is very unlike the "Bear and forbear" (*sustine et abstine*) of the stoic. The saint tells his disciples what he tells himself: "Mistrust a state of hopelessness and depression, because you are then under the influence of a bad spirit, but when your heart is light and you feel strong and joyous, go forward, for God is with you." Is not this the best possible incentive to action? For it is surely better to begin by resolute action which is in time reinforced by a feeling of manly joy, than to start with a feeling of pleasure which is likely to become insipid and to weaken the energy of the soul.

To come now to a practical conclusion: we must make profit out of desolation as out of any other punishment, trial or lesson, but we must also fight against it by means of reflection and prayer and still more by constancy to former resolutions made in time of consolation. From a merely human point of view, this rule, if followed, must carry us victorious through useless regrets and moments of weakness. It is to no purpose to object that there is danger of confounding consolation and illusion, and that desolation may sometimes be only a clearer sight of real difficulties and obstacles, for the saints do not fall into either of these errors. They have entertained preliminary doubts when these were in any way reasonable, for, as the Scriptures tell us, there is a time for all things, a time for hesitation and a time for decision. If there are difficulties when the time comes for execution, there is all the greater need of prudence and earnest prayer, not indeed for the purpose of reopening the whole question, but in order to obtain fresh light and strength which will enable the soul to bring the work which it has begun to a successful issue. Thanks to habits like these, nothing is lost of the energy generated by the presence of faith, hope and charity in the soul. Nothing is left to work itself off in sadness and doubt. It is all spent and at the same time renewed by firm and confident action.

This is what makes the optimism of the saints, which is the only reasonable kind of optimism, the greatest force which the world has ever known.

And how does it employ itself? The works of charity scattered over the globe proclaim the answer to this question, and they would proclaim it even more loudly did the world not reject the love of God's servants. St Bernard describes the active life as follows: The active life consists in giving bread to those who have none, in teaching the word of wisdom to our neighbour, in bringing back into the right path those who have gone astray, in recalling the proud to charity and enemies to peace and concord, in visiting the sick and burying the dead, in ransoming captives and prisoners, and in seeing that each one has what he requires." (Treatise on the way to live a good life.)

What a field of action the above programme opens out to the saints of all ages, including—if we may be allowed to say so—the saints of the future! Giving bread to those who have none, means more than a trifling charity. It means organising works and

FEELING, LOVE AND ACTION 179

creating methods of association, as well as exercising forethought, so that each man's daily sustenance may be secured to him. Visiting the sick means causing charity to co-operate with the science of medicine and surgery, so that the wonderful power possessed by the latter may not, as is often the case, be nullified by the carelessness and misery with which it has to cope. Making peace means a restoration of those relations which once enabled pastors of souls to intervene for the preservation of the peace of families and Christian states, and which would empower them to disarm ruthless competition by enjoining everywhere the *bona fide* practice of such conditions as would ensure a reasonable, humane and moderate amount of labour. The number of captives and prisoners to console increases in the prisons in proportion to the growing number of criminals who work for the universal destruction of society. A saint who would found an Order recognised by civil society might, in these days, effect the conversion of these offenders and prepare them to become useful members of a society which, as things are now, only seeks to get rid of them after having made them what they are.

Such is the active life of the servant of God, and he has need of all the light, all the purity, reflection, love and spirit of self-sacrifice, as well as of all the joy of which, as we have seen, the saint's soul is capable, to enable him to support the weight of his increasing labours.

Two orders of evolution are working themselves out on the earth. One of them is briefly described by Ignatius of Loyola, under these three heads: the Flesh, the World, and Satan. The Flesh, with its lusts and its tendency to animal gratifications—The World, with its rivalries, quarrels and hatreds—Satan is the exterior suggestion to every one of those cries which appeal to us and endeavour to enslave us to our ruin.

The whole secret of the life of sanctity may be summed up under three very opposite heads: the Spirit, the Church, and Christ. The Spirit, which is the master and controller of the Flesh which has been reduced to its proper and subordinate condition—the Church, which unites together all men of good will—Christ, our eternal model in whom we are brought face to face with our own humanity, restored and glorified.

APPENDIX

Page 6. It may be contested whether ὁσιότης, as defined and described in the *Euthyphro*, corresponds exactly to our English sense of the word sanctity. So far as it only implies an obedient fulfilment of the divine law, a loyal rendering of all religious dues, it scarcely goes beyond piety (*pietas*), or 'religion' in the sense of religiousness. But it can hardly be denied that in this dialogue, and more explicitly elsewhere, ὁσιότης is considered to involve a certain likeness to the gods, a sharing of their nature and contemplative beatitude which is very analogous to the Christian notion of saintliness. At all events M. Joly does not contend that the special Christian conception, but only that the generic conception of sanctity is common to all religions of note.

Page 38. Of course this proposition is not convertible. 'Mysticism is the love of God'; but not all love of God is mysticism, though indeed it contains the rudiments or elements of mysticism in so far as all love, both human and divine, is a principle of life and conduct which refuses the analysis of reason, having instincts and intentions which enable it to leap to conclusions, speculative as well as practical, to which reason can never even crawl. Still the word 'mysticism' is reserved by usage for an unwonted degree of such unitive insight, just as sanctity is used only of extraordinary degrees of sanctification, and heroism for a fortitude which seems superhuman.

Page 76. Our attention was called only at the last moment to the error by which a letter of S. Francis of Sales (see "Letters of S. Francis of Sales to Persons in the World"; translated by Rev. Fr. H. B. Mackey, O.S.B.—Book V. Letter XVII.) has here been ascribed to S. Jane de Chantal.

Page 91. That is, of course, if we assume what we need not

assume, namely, the objectivity of such apparitions. It is plainly indifferent whether the miracle be worked in the mind and consciousness of the assembled crowd or in order of things external to their mind, since there is no question of a reality, but only of an appearance.

Page 99. In other words the higher vocation is the harder, and the percentage of those who fail in it greater. Ampler faculties and graces are not only apt but more liable to be diverted to greater ruin. This is in the very nature of things and it is useless to complain. An heresiarch or schismatic is often only a reformer soured and gone bad through anger, impatience, pride, failure of faith. Moses trembled on the verge once or twice; Savonarola more than trembled. God has a fair thought to utter in each man's life, but if it be mouthed and marred in the utterance, then is the discord shrill and strident with all the strength that was lent for harmony.

Page 127. It is chiefly in its milder and more human conception of the relation of the body to the soul, and consequently of the senses and imagination to the intellect, of the passions and emotions to the will, that the peripatetic philosophy is more in harmony with the economy of the Incarnation than the platonic. The latter is perhaps a more apt medium for expressing those dogmas which concern the mysteries of the divinity and of the purely spiritual order. The Christian religion has availed herself of both one and the other according as she has found them in common vogue. She commits herself to no sect or school of philosophy except in respect to those common principles which are the necessary product of the human mind; but she uses philosophies as she uses languages, to translate divine truths into them as accurately as the limits of language will permit, and so to convey her mysteries to the human mind of every age and country whatever be its tongue, whatever its forms of thought, its science, its tradition, history, and legendary lore.

Page 137. It may be remarked that the whole scope and end of that course of spiritual treatment to which St Ignatius of Loyola subjects the soul during the weeks of "the Exercises" is to secure a state of interior calm and indifference in order that the retreatant may be able to make an election, either as to some particular

APPENDIX 183

crisis or as to his general course of life, unbiassed by any excessive like or dislike, and guided solely by the consideration of what will most conduce to the one end for which he was created—the glory of God and the perfection of his own soul. "Spiritual Exercises," he titles them, "that a man may set his life in order without therein being determined by any disorderly affection."

Page 140. Whatever may be true of the percentage, it is certainly not true that religious orders have produced absolutely more saints than the secular state. If we speak of canonised saints, *i.e.*, of that small handful whose sanctity has by one circumstance or another been brought under public gaze, it may well be that a religious corporation will have the means and the motive for forwarding a *process* which in other circumstances would never have been heard of. Similarly, among canonised saints the proportion of bishops to priests is very large, doubtless because a bishop's office brings him into greater prominence and affords opportunity for more striking action. Finally, against all our antecedent expectations, the number of canonised men saints is large compared with that of women; but plainly for just the same reason.

Page 152. There is much curious reading on this subject, such as would have delighted Charles Lamb, in the first section of the second part of the 'Summa' of Aquinas,[1] which shows that it was due rather to the defective instruments and methods at their disposal than to any lack of observation or industry that the all-inquiring schoolmen failed in the details of their physiology of the emotions, while anticipating many of the leading ideas and principles of the modern psychologists.

Page 166. It is much to be regretted that certain recent controversies should have revealed a disposition on the part of some to credit the Catholic religion with the sentiments and practices of individuals or even nationalities professing that creed. This is plainly illiberal and witless, unless it can be shown that such sentiments are the product and logical outcome of Catholic beliefs and principles. It may well be that in combating the extravagances

[1] Qq. 28, 33, 44, 48, etc. of *Aquinas Ethicus*, translated by Rev. J. Rickaby, S. J.

of a purely emotional and unreasoning zoophily which is anxious about vegetable boots and miteless cheese, and tends to deny any special sacredness to human life which does equally belong to "everything that hath breath," the apologists of sound sense have insisted too exclusively on the negative side of animals 'rights,' leaving the positive to take care of itself; it may be that they have couched their arguments in a philosophy and terminology not "understanded of a people" at best impatient of any philosophy; but this is an evil incident to every controversy and for which the assailants and not the defenders of the received position are answerable. Not only is there nothing in the principles of Catholic teaching to countenance brutality or carelessness in regard to animal suffering, but there is everything to encourage a rational carefulness and consideration. It should however be observed that a sensitive sympathy with physical suffering is a growth of civilisation involving a high development of the imagination and a delicacy of the nervous system which we seek in vain in savage or semi-barbarised peoples; and which it is not one of the direct effects of religion as such to produce. What seems to be, and in us would be, cruelty, is in the animal or the child or the savage mere bluntness of perception and coarseness of nerve. This explains how those who are so kind and sympathetic in some respects (namely, in regard to sufferings they perceive and understand) are so seemingly heartless in others. It is not wonderful then that those who in a way are good Christians and kindly to their fellows should often exhibit brutality in their treatment of animals, as is to be seen so commonly in Italy. It is a defect of civilisation rather than of religion whose action on civilisation is always indirect and often impeded by other conditions over which it has no control. G. T.

Made in the USA
Monee, IL
31 March 2023